THE DEVELOPMENT OF METAPHYSICS IN PERSIA

A CONTRIBUTION TO THE HISTORY
OF
MUSLIM PHILOSOPHY

BY
MUHAMMAD IQBAL

FOREWORD

This work is Iqbal's first philosophical attempt and, therefore, is not free from the marks of immaturity; and yet until it is superseded by a more comprehensive work, it will retain its importance in Oriental studies. It was written at a time when he was an admirer of pantheism—a world view which he completely repudiated a few years later. That is why he has spoken in the introduction in such glowing terms of Ibn-al-Arabi, has given in the text practically no place to his future teacher and guide, Jalal-al-Din Rumi, and has paid more attention to the treatment of Pantheistic Sufiism than to any other philosophical school. In his observations regarding Al-Farabi, Ibn-Maskwaih and Ibn-Sina, he has more or less echoed the views of early Western Orientalists and has denied these great thinkers the credit for originality and deviation from Neo-Platonism. There is no doubt that if he were to re-write this work, he would have differently evaluated their philosophical efforts and would have also given to Rumi's thought the extensive treatment it really deserved.

However, this work presents the first and the only historical account of Persia's philosophical thought and the credit of its conception goes to Iqbal. He has successfully examined both Persian Idealism and Realism and in his analysis of the conditions that led to the rise of Sufiism, he has corrected the mistakes of his predecessors. For a work of this type, the author must combine in himself scholarship in at least two Oriental languages, Persian and Arabic, in one or more European languages, and in the History of Philosophy, Eastern and Western. These qualifications were pre-eminently held by Iqbal, and therefore he achieved what no one without these qualifications could achieve. Besides, in representing, as it does, the first stage of Iqbal's development, this treatise is of great value to the students of Iqbal's own speculation. The Bazm-i-Iqbal has, therefore, done these students a service in placing in their hands this second edition.

M. M. SHARIF

DEDICATION

TO

PROFESSOR T. W. ARNOLD, M.A.

My dear Mr. Arnold,

This little book is the first fruit of that literary and philosophical training, which I have been receiving from you for the last ten years, and as an expression of gratitude, I beg to dedicate it to your name. You have always judged me liberally ; I hope you will judge these pages in the same spirit.

Your affectionate pupil

Iqbal.

CONTENTS

PART I
PRE-ISLAMIC PERSIAN PHILOSOPHY

		Page
Chapter I	Persian Dualism	3
	1. Zoroaster	3
	3. Mānī and Mazdak	11
	3. Retrospect	17

PART II
GREEK DUALISM

Chapter II	Neo-Platonic Aristotelians of Persia	21
	1. Ibn Maskawaih	23
	2. Avicenna	32
Chapter III	Islamic Rationalism	38
	1. Metaphysics of Rationalism—Materialism	38
	2. Contemporary Movements of Thought	45
	3. Reaction against Rationalism—The Ash'arite	52
Chapter IV	Controversy between Realism and Idealism	65
Chapter V	Ṣūfīism	76
	1. The origin and Quranic Justification of Ṣūfīism	76
	2. Aspects of Ṣūfī Metaphysics	87
	A. Reality as Self-conscious Will	87
	B. Reality as Beauty	88
	C. (1) Reality as Light	94
	(Return to Persian Dualism—Al-Ishrāqī)	
	(2) Reality as Thought—Al-Jīlī	116
Chapter VI	Later Persian Thought	134
Conclusion		147

INTRODUCTION

The most remarkable feature of the character of the Persian people is their love of Metaphysical speculation. Yet the inquirer who approaches the extant literature of Persia expecting to find any comprehensive systems of thought, like those of Kapila or Kant, will have to turn back disappointed, though deeply impressed by the wonderful intellectual subtlety displayed therein. It seems to me that the Persian mind is rather impatient of detail, and consequently destitute of that organising faculty which gradually works out a system of ideas, by interpreting the fundamental principles with reference to the ordinary facts of observation. The subtle Brahman sees the inner unity of things ; so does the Persian. But while the former endeavours to discover it in all the aspects of human experience, and illustrates its hidden presence in the concrete in various ways, the latter appears to be satisfied with a bare universality, and does not attempt to verify the richness of its inner content. The butterfly imagination of the Persian, flies half-inebriated as it were, from flower to flower, and seems to be incapable of reviewing the garden as a whole. For this reason, his deepest thoughts and emotions find expression mostly in disconnected verses (Ghazal), which reveal all the subtlety of his artistic soul. The Hindū, while admitting, like the Persian, the necessity of a higher source of knowledge, yet calmly moves from experience to experience, mercilessly dissecting them, and forcing them to yield their underlying universality. In fact the Persian is only half-conscious of Metaphysics as a *system* of thought; his Brahman brother, on the other hand, is fully alive to the need of presenting his theory in the form of a thoroughly reasoned out system. And the result of this mental difference between the two nations is clear. In the one case we have only partially worked out systems of thought : in the other case, the awful sublimity of the searching Vedānta. The student of Islamic Mysticism who is anxious to see an all-embracing exposition of the principle of Unity, must look up the heavy volumes of the Andalūsian Ibn al-'Arabī, whose profound teaching stands in strange contrast with the dry-as-dust Islām of his countrymen.

The results, however, of the intellectual activity of the different branches of the great Aryan family are strikingly similar. The outcome of all Idealistic speculation in India is Buddha, in Persia Bahāullah, and in the west Schopenhauer whose system, in Hegelian language, is the marriage of free oriental universality with occidental determinateness.

But the history of Persian thought presents a phenomenon peculiar to itself. In Persia, due perhaps to Semitic influences, philosophical speculation has indissolubly associated itself with religion, and thinkers in new lines of thought have almost always been founders of new religious movements. After the Arab conquest, however, we see pure Philosophy severed from religion by the Neo-Platonic Aristotelians of Islām, but the severance was only a transient phenomenon. Greek philosophy, though an exotic plant in the soil of Persia, eventually became an integral part of Persian thought; and later thinkers, critics as well as advocates of Greek wisdom, talked in the philosophical language of Aristotle and Plato, and were mostly influenced by religious pre-suppositions. It is necessary to bear this fact in mind in order to gain a thorough understanding of post-Islamic Persian thought.

The object of this investigation is, as will appear, to prepare a ground-work for a future history of Persian Metaphysics. Original thought cannot be expected in a review, the object of which is purely historical; yet I venture to claim some consideration for the following two points :—

(a) I have endeavoured to trace the logical continuity of Persian thought, which I have tried to interpret in the language of modern Philosophy. This, as far as I know, has not yet been done.

(b) I have discussed the subject of Sufiism in a more scientific manner, and have attempted to bring out the intellectual conditions which necessitated such a phenomenon. In opposition, therefore, to the generally accepted view I have tried to maintain that Sufiism is a necessary product of the play of various intellectual and moral forces which would necessarily awaken the slumbering soul to a higher ideal of life.

Owing to my ignorance of Zend, my knowledge of Zoroaster is merely second-hand. As regards the second part of my work, I have been able to look up the original Persian and Arabic manuscripts as well as many printed works connected with my investigation. I give below the names of Arabic and Persian manuscripts from which I have drawn most of the material utilized here. The method of transliteration adopted is the one recognised by the Royal Asiatic Society.

1. Tarikl al-Hukamā, by ʿAl-Baihaqī,—Rayal Library of Berlin.
2. Sharhi Anwāriyya, (with the original text) by Muhammad Sharīf of Herāt, ,,
3. Hikmat al-ʿAin, by al-Kātibī. .,
4. Commentary on Hikmat al-ʿAin, by Muhammad ibn Mubārak al-Bukhārī—India Office Library.
5. Commentary on Hikmat al-ʿAin by Husainī. ,,
6. ʿAwārif al-Maʿārif, by Shahāb al-Dīn, ,,
7. Mishkāt al-Anwār, by Al-Ghazālī. ,,
8. Kashf al-Mahjūb, by ʿAlī Hajverī. ,,
9. Risālahi Nafs, translated from Aristotle, by Afḍal Kāshī. ,,
10. Risālahi Mir Sayyid Sharif. ,,
11. Khātima, by Sayyid Muhammad Gisūdarāz. ,,
12. Manāzilal-saʾrīn, by Abdullah Ismāiʾl of Herāt. ,,
13. Jāwidān Nāma, by Afḍal Kāshī. ,,
14. Tārikh al-Hukamā, by Shahizūrī. Britsh Museum Library.
15. Collected Works of Avicenna. ,,
16. Risalah fiʾl-Wujūd, by Mir Jurjānī ,,
17. Jāwidāni Kabīr, Cambridge University Library.
18. Jāmi Jahān Numā ,,
19. Majmuʿai Fārsi Risālah Nos : 1, 2, of Al-Nasafī. Trinity College Library.

S. M. IQBAL.

PART I
PRE-ISLAMIC PERSIAN PHILOSOPHY

CHAPTER I

PERSIAN DUALISM

1. ZOROASTER

To Zoroaster—the ancient sage of Iran—must always be assigned the first place in the intellectual history of Iranian Aryans who, wearied of constant roaming, settled down to an agricultural life at a time when the Vedic Hymns were still being composed in the plains of Central Asia. This new mode of life and the consequent stability of the institution of property among the settlers, made them hated by other Aryan tribes who had not yet shaken off their original nomadic habits, and occasionally plundered their more civilised kinsmen. Thus grew up the conflict between the two modes of life which found its earliest expression in the denunciation of the deities of each other—the Devas and the Ahuras. It was really the beginning of a long individualising process which gradually severed the Iranian branch from other Aryan tribes, and finally manifested itself in the religious system of Zoroaster[1]—the

---

[1] Some European scholars have held Zoroaster to be nothing more than a mythical personage. But since the publication of Professor Jackson's admirable *Life of Zoroaster*, the Iranian Prophet has, I believe, finally got out of the ordeal of modern criticism.

great prophet of Iran who lived and taught in the age of Solon and Thales. In the dim light of modern oriental research we see ancient Iranians divided between two camps—partisans of the powers of good, and partisans of the powers of evil—when the great sage joins their furious contest, and with his moral enthusiasm stamps out once for all the worship of demons as well as the intolerable ritual of the Magian priesthood.

It is, however, beside our purpose to trace the origion and growth of Zoroaster's religious system. Our object, in so far as the present investigation is concerned, is to glance at the metaphysical side of his revelation. We, therefore, wish to fix our attention on the sacred trinity of philosophy—God, Man and Nature.

Geiger, in his "Civilisation of Eastern Iranians in Ancient Times", points out that Zoroaster inherited two fundamental principles from his Aryan ancestry :— (1) There is law in Nature. (2) There is conflict in Nature. It is the observation of law and conflict in the vast panorama of being that constitutes the philosophical foundation of his system. The problem before him was to reconcile the existance of evil with the eternal goodness of God. His predecessors worshipped a plurality of good spirits all of which he reduced to a unity and called it Ahuramazda. On the other hand he reduced all the powers of evil to a similar unity and called it Druj-Ahriman. Thus by a process of unification he arrived at two fundamental principles which, as

Haug shows, he looked upon not as two independent activities, but as two parts or rather aspects of the same Primary Being. Dr. Haug, therefore, holds that the Prophet of ancient Iran was theologically a monotheist and philosophically a dualist.[1] But to maintain that there are "twin"[2] spirits—creators of reality and nonreality—and at the same time to hold that these two spirits are united in the Supreme Being,[3] is virtually to say that the principle of evil constitutes a part of the very essence of God; and the conflict between good and evil is nothing more than the struggle of God against Himself. There is therefore, an inherent weakness in his attempt to reconcile theological monotheism with philosophical dualism, and the result was a schism among the prophet's followers. The Zendiks[4] whom Dr. Haug calls heretics, but who were, I believe, decidedly more consistent than their opponents, maintained the independence of the two original spirits from each other, while the Magi upheld their unity. The upholders of unity endeavoured, in various ways, to meet the Zendiks; but the very fact that they tried different phrases and expressions to express the unity of the "Primal Twins", indicates dissatisfaction with their own philosophical explanations, and the

[1] Essays, p. 303.
[2] "In the beginning there was a pair of twins, two spirits, each of a peculiar activity." Yas. XXX. 1.
[3] "The more beneficial of my spirits has produced, by speaking it, the whole rightful creation." Yas. XIX. 9.
[4] The following verse from Buudahísh Chap. I, will indicate the Zendik view :— "And between them (the two principles) there was empty space, that is what they call "air" in which is now their meeting."

strength of their opponent's position. Shahrastāni[1] describes briefly the different explanations of the Magi. The Zarwānians look upon Light and Darkness as the sons of Infinite Time. The Kiyūmarthiyya hold that the original principle was Light which was afraid of a hostile power, and it was this thought of adversary mixed with fear that led to the birth of Darkness. Another branch of Zarwānians maintain that the original principle doubted concerning something and this doubt produced Ahriman. Ibn Hazm[2] speaks of another sect who explained the principle of Darkness as the obscuration of a part of the fundamental principle of Light itself.

Whether the philosophical dualism of Zoroaster can be reconciled with his monotheism or not, it is unquestionable that, from a metaphysical standpoint, he has made a profound suggestion in regard to the ultimate nature of reality. The idea seems to have influenced ancient Greek Philosophy[3] as well as early

[1] Shahrastānī : ed. Cureton, London, 1846, pp. 182—185.
[2] Ibn Hazm—Kitāb al-Milal w'al-Nihal ; ed. Cairo, Vol. 11, p. 34.
[3] In connection with the influence of Zoroastrian ideas on Ancient Greek thought, the following statement made by Erdmann is noteworthy, though Lawrence Mills (American Journal of Philology, Vol. 22) regards such influence as improbable :— "The fact that the handmaids of this force, which he (Heraclitus) calls the seed of all that happens and the measure of all order, are entitled the "tongues" has probably been slightly ascribed to the influence of the Persian Magi. On the other hand he connects himself with his country's mythology, not indeed without a change of exegesis when he places Apollo and Dionysus beside Zeus, i.e. The ultimate fire, as the two aspects of his nature". History of Philosophy, Vol. 1, p. 50.
It is, perhaps, owing to this doubtful influence of Zoroastrianism on Heraclitus that Lassalle (quoted by Paul Janet in his History of the Problems of Philosophy, Vol. 11 p. 147) looks upon Zaroaster as a precursor of Hegel.

Christian Gnostic speculation, and through the latter, some aspects of modern Western thought.[1] As a thinker he is worthy of great respect not only because he approached the problem of objective multiplicity in a philosophical spirit, but also because he endeavoured, having been led to metaphysical dualism, to reduce his Primary Duality to higher unity. He seems to have perceived, what the mystic shoemaker of Germany perceived long after him, that the diversity of nature could not be explained without postulating a principle of negativity or self-differentiation in the very nature of God. His immediate successors did not, however, quite realise the deep significance of their master's suggestions ; but we shall see, as we advance, how Zoroaster's idea finds a more spiritualised expression in some of the aspects of later Persian thought.

Of Zoroastrian influence on Pythagoras, Erdmann says :—

"The fact that the odd numbers are put above the even, has een emphasised by Gladisch in his comparison of the Pythagorian with the Chinese doctrine, and the fact, moreover, that among the oppositions we find those of light and darkness, good and evil, has induced many, in ancient and modern times, to suppose that they were borrowed from Zoroastrianism." Vol. I, p. 33.

[1] Among modern English thinkers Mr. Bradley arrives at a conclusion similar to that of Zoroaster. Discussing the ethical significance of Bradley's Philosophy, Prof. Sorley says :— "Mr. Bradley, like Green, has faith in an eternal reality which might be called spiritual, inasmuch as it is not material ; like Green, he looks upon man's moral activity as an appearance—what Green calls a reproduction—of this eternal reality. But under this general agreement there lies a world of difference. He refuses by the use of the term self-conscious, to liken his Absolute to the personality of man, and he brings out the consequence which in Green is more or less concealed, that the evil equally with the good in man and in the world are appearances of the Absolute". Recent Tendencies in Ethics, pp. 100-101.

Turning now to his Cosmology, his dualism leads him to bifurcate, as it were, the whole universe into two departments of being—reality i.e. the sum of all good creations flowing from the creative activity of the beneficial spirit, and non-reality[1] i.e. the sum of all evil creations proceeding from the hostile spirit. The original conflict of the two spirits is manifested in the opposing forces of nature, which, therefore, presents a continual struggle between the powers of Good and the powers of Evil. But it should be remembered that nothing intervenes between the original spirits and their respective creations. Things are good and bad because they proceed from good or bad creative agencies, in their own nature they are quite indifferent. Zoroaster's conception of creation is fundamentally different from that of Plato and Schopenhauer to whom spheres of empirical reality reflect non-temporal or temporal ideas which, so to speak, mediate between Reality and Appearance. There are, according to Zoroaster, only two categories of existence, and the history of the universe is nothing more than a progressive conflict between the forces falling respectively under these categories. We are, like other things, partakers of this struggle, and it is our duty to range ourselves on the side of Light which will eventually prevail and completely vanquish the spirit of Darkness. The metaphysics of the Iranian Prophet, like

[1] This should not be confounded with Plato's non-being. To Zoroaster all forms of existence proceeding from the creative agency of the spirit of darkness are unreal; because, considering the final triumph of the spirit of Light, they have a temporary existence only.

that of Plato, passes on into Ethics, and it is in the peculiarity of the Ethical aspect of his thought that the influence of his social environment is most apparent.

Zoroaster's view of the destiny of the soul is very simple. The soul, according to him, is a creation, not a part of God as the votaries of Mithra[1] afterwards maintained. It had a beginning in time, but can attain to everlasting life by fighting against Evil in the earthly scene of its activity. It is free to choose between the only two courses of action—good and evil; and besides the power of choice the spirit of Light has endowed it with the following faculties :—

1. Conscience[2].
2. Vital force.
3. The Soul—The Mind.
4. The Spirit—Reason.
5. The Farāwashi[3]—A kind of tutelary spirit which acts as a protection of man in his voyage towards God.

---

[1] Mithraism was a phase of Zoroastrianism which spread over the Roman world in the second century. The partisans of Mithra worshipped the sun whom they looked upon as the great advocate of Light. They held the human soul to be a part of God, and maintained that the observance of a mysterious cult could bring about the soul's union with God. Their doctrine of the soul, its ascent towards God by torturing the body and finally passing through the sphere of Aether and becoming pure fire, offers some resemblance with views entertained by some schools of Persian Sufiism.

[2] Geiger's "Civilisation of Eastern Iranians", Vol. I, p. 124.

[3] Dr. Haug (Essays, p. 205) compares these protecting spirits with the ideas of Plato. They, however, are not to be under-

The last three[1] facultries are united together after death, and form an indissoluble whole. The virtuous soul, leaving its home of flesh, is borne up into higher regions, and has to pass through the following planes of existence :—

1. The Place of good thoughts.
2. The Place of good words.
3. The Place of good works.
4. The Place of Eternal Glory[2].—Where the

stood as models according to which things are fashioned. Plato's ideas, moreover, are eternal, non-temporal and non-spatial. The doctrine that everything created by the spirit of Light is protected by a subordinate spirit, has only an outward resemblance with the view that every spirit is fashioned according to a perfect supersensible model.

[1] The Sūfī conception of the soul is also tripartite. According to them the soul is a combination of Mind, Heart and Spirit (Nafs, Qalb, Rūh). The "heart" is to them both material and immaterial or, more properly, neither—standing midway between soul and mind (Nafs and Rūh), and acting as the organ of 'higher knowledge". Perhaps Dr. Schenkel's use of the word "conscience" would approach the sūfī idea of "heart".

[2] Geiger, Vol. I, p. 104. The sūfī Cosmology has a similar doctrine concerning the different stages of existence through which the soul has to pass in its journey heavenward. They enumerate the following five Planes ; but their definition of the character of each plane is slightly different :—

1. The world of body (Nāsūt).
2. The world of pure intelligence (Malakūt).
3. The world of power (Jabrūt).
4. The world of negation (Lāhūt).
5. The world of Absolute Silence (Hāhūt).

The sūfīs probably borrowed this idea from the Indian Yogīs who recognise the following seven Planes :—(Annie Besant : "Reincarnation", p. 30).

1. The Plane of Physical Body.
2. The Plane of Etherial Double.
3. The Plane of Vitality.

individual soul unites with the principle of Light without losing its personality.

2. MANI[1] AND MAZDAK[2]

We have seen Zoroaster's solution of the problem of diversity, and the theological or rather philosophical controversy which split up the Zoroastrian Church. The half-Persian Māni—"the founder of Godless community" as Christians styled him afterwards—agrees with those Zoroastrians who held their Prophet's doctrine in its naked form, and approaches the question in a spirit thoroughly materialistic. Originally Persian, his father emigrated from Hamadān to Babylonia where Māni was born in 215

    4. The Plane of Emotional Nature.
    5. The Plane of Thought.
    6. The Plane of Spiritual soul—Reason.
    7. The Plane of Pure Spirit.

[1]Sources used :—
(a) The text of Muhammad ibn Ishāq, edited by Flügel, pp. 52—56.
(b) Al-Ya'qūbī : ed. Houtsma, 1883, Vol. I, pp. 180-181.
(c) Ibn Hazm : Kitāb al-Milal w'al-Nihal : ed. Cairo, Vol. II, p. 36.

    Shahrastānī : ed. Cureton, London, 1846, pp. 188—192.
    Encyclopædia Britannica Article on Māni.
    Salemann : Bulletin de l'Académie des Sciences de St. Petersburg Series IV, 15, April 1907, pp. 175—184. F. W. K. Muller ; Handschriften—Reste in Estrangelo—Schrift aus Turfan, Chinesisch—Turkistan, Teil I, II ; Sitzungen der Königlich Preussischen Akademie der Wissenschaften, 11 Feb, 1904, pp. 348—352 ; un Abhandlungen etc. 1904.

[2]Sources used :—
(a) Siyāsat Nāmah Nizām al-Mulk : ed. Charles Schefer, Paris. 1897 pp. 166—181.
(b) Shahrastānī : ed. Cureton, pp 192—194.
(c) Al-Ya'qūbī ; ed. Houtsma, 1883, Vol. I, p. 186.
(d) Al-Bīrūnī : Chronology of Ancient Nations : tr. E. Sachau, London, 1879, p. 192.

or 216 A.D.—the time when Buddhistic Missionaries were beginning to preach Nirvāna to the country of Zoroaster. The electic character of the religious system of Mānī, its bold extension of the Christian idea of redemption, and its logical consistency in holding, as a true ground for an ascetic life, that the world is essentially evil, made it a real power which influenced not only Eastern and Western Christian thought[1], but has also left some dim marks on the development of metaphysical speculation in Persia. Leaving the discussion of the sources[2] of Mānī's religious system to the orientalist, we proceed to describe and finally to determine the philosophical value of his doctrine of the origin of the Phenomenal Universe.

The Paganising gnostic, as Erdmann calls him, teaches that the variety of things springs from the

[1] "If I see aright, five different conceptions can be distinguished for the period about 400 A.D. First we have the Manichaean which insinuated its way in the darkness, but was widely extended even among the clergy". (Harnack's "History of Christian Dogma," Vol. V, p. 56). "From the anti-Manichaean controversy sprang the desire to conceive all God's attributes as identical i.e. the interest in the indivisibility of God." (ibid. Vol. V, p. 120).

[2] Some Eastern sources of information about Mānī's Philosophy (e.g. Ephraim Syrus mentioned by Prof. A. A. Bevan in his Introduction to the Hymn of the soul) tell us that he was a disciple of Bardesanes, the Syrian gnostic. The learned author of "al Fihrist", however, mentions some books which Mānī wrote against the followers of the Syrian gnostic. Burkitt, in his lectures on Early Eastern Christianity, gives a free translation of Bardesanes' *De Fato*, the spirit of which I understand, is fully Christian, and thoroughly opposed to the teaching of Mānī. Ibn Hazm, however, in his Kitāb al-Milal w'al-Niḥal (Vol. II, p. 36) says, "Both agreed in other respects, except that Mānī believed darkness to be a living principle."

mixture of two eternal Principles—Light and Darkness—which are separate from and independent of each other. The Principle of Light connotes ten ideas—Gentleness, Knowledge, Understanding, Mystery, Insight, Love, Conviction, Faith, Benevolence and Wisdom. Similarly the Principle of Darkness connotes five eternal ideas—Mistiness, Heat, Fire, Venom, Darkness. Along with these two primordial principles and connected with each, Mānī recognises the eternity of space and earth, each connoting respectively the ideas of knowledge, understanding, mystery, insight, breath, air, water, light and fire. In darkness—the feminine Principle in Nature—were hidden the elements of evil which, in the course of time, concentrated and resulted in the composition, so to speak, of the hideous-looking Devil—the principle of factivity. This first-born child of the fiery womb of darkness attacked the domain of the King of Light who, in order to ward off his malicious onslaught, created the Primal man. A serious conflict ensued between the two creatures, and resulted in the complete vanquishment of the Primal man. The evil one, then, succeeded in mixing together the five elements of darkness with the five elements of light. Thereupon the ruler of the domain of light ordered some of his angels to construct the Universe out of these mixed elements with a view to free the atoms of light from their imprisonment. But the reason why darkness was the first to attack light, is that the latter, being in its essence good, could not proceed to start the process of admixture which was essentially harmful to itself. The attitude of Māni's Cosmology, therefore, to the Christian doctrine of Redemption is similar to that of Hegelian Cosmology to the doctrine of the Trinity. To him redemption is a physical process and all procreation, because it protracts the imprisonment of light, is contrary to the aim and object of the Universe. The imprisoned atoms of light are continually set free from darkness which is thrown down in the unfathomable ditch round the Universe. The liberated light, however, passes on to the sun and the moon whence it is carried by angels to the region of light—the eternal home of the King of Paradise—"Pīd i vazargīi"—Father of greatness.

This is a brief account of Māni's fantastic Cosmology.[1] He rejects the Zoroastrian hypothesis of creative agencies to explain the problem of objective existence. Taking a thoroughly materialistic view of the question, he ascribes the phenomenal universe to the *Mixture* of two independent, eternal principles, one of which (darkness) is not only a part of the universe—stuff, but also the source wherein activity resides, as it were, slumbering, and starts up into being when the favourable moment arrives. The essential idea of his cosmology, therefore, has a curious resemblance with that of the great Hindū

[1] It is interesting to compare Māni's Philosophy of Nature with the Chinese notion of Creation, according to which all that exists flows from the Union of Yin and Yang. But the Chinese reduced these two principles to a higher unity :— Tai Keih. To Māni such a reduction was not possible ; since he could not conceive that things of opposite nature could proceed from the same principle.

thinker Kapila, who accounts for the production of the universe by the hypothesis of three gunas, i.e. Sattwa (goodness), Tamas (darkness), and Rajas (motion or passion) which mix together to form Nature, when the equilibrium of the primordial matter (Prakriti) is upset. Of the various solutions[1] of the problem of diversity which the Vedantist solved by postulating the mysterious power of "Maya", and Leibniz, long afterwards, explained by his doctrine of the Identity of Indiscernibles, Mani's solution, though childish, must find a place in the historical development of philosophical ideas. Its philosophical value may be insignificant ; but one thing is certain, i.e. Mani was the first to venture the suggestion that the Universe is due to the activity of the Devil, and hence essentially evil—a proposition which seems to me to be the only logical justification of a system which preaches renunciation as the guiding principle of life. In our own times, Schopenhauer has been led to the same conclusion ;

[1]Thomas Aquinas states and criticises Mani's contrariety of Primal agents in the following manner :—
    (a) What all things seek even a principle of evil would seek.
        But all things seek their own self-preservation.
∴ Even a principle of evil would seek its own self-preservation.
    (b) What all things seek is good.
        But self-preservation is what all things seek.
∴ Self-preservation is good.
        But a principle of evil would seek its own self-preservation.
∴ A principle of evil would seek some good—which shows that it is self-contradictory.
    God and His Creatures, Book II, p. 105. Rickaby's Tr.

though, unlike Māni, he supposes the principle of objectification or individuation—"the sinful bent" of the will to life—to exist in the very nature of the Primal Will and not independent of it.

Turning now to the remarkable socialist of ancient Persia—*Mazdak*. This early prophet of communism appeared during the reign of Anūshirwān the Just (531—578 A D.), and marked another dualistic reaction against the prevailing Zarwānian doctrine[1]. Mazdak, like Māni, taught that the diversity of things springs from the mixture of two independent, eternal principles which he called Shīd (Light) and Tār (Darkness). But he differs from his predecessor in holding that the fact of their mixture as well as their final separation, are quite accidental, and not at all the result of choice, Mazdak's God is endowed with sensation, and has four principal energies in his eternal presence—power of discrimination, memory, understanding and bliss. These four energies have four personal manifestations who, assisted by four other persons, superintend the course of the Universe. Variety in things and men is due to the various combinations of the original principles.

But the most characteristic feature of the Mazdakite teaching is its communism, which is evidently an inference from the cosmopolitan spirit of Māni's Philosophy. All men, said Mazdak, are equal; and the notion of individual property was

[1] The Zarwānian doctrine prevailed in Persia in the 5th century B. C. (See Z. D. M. G., Vol. LVII, p. 562.)

introduced by the hostile demons whose object is to turn God's Universe into a scene of endless misery. It is chiefly this aspect of Mazdak's teaching that was most shocking to the Zoroastrian conscience, and finally brought about the destruction of his enormous following, even though the master was supposed to have miraculously made the sacred Fire talk, and bear witness to the truth of his mission.

3. RETROSPECT

We have seen some of the aspects of Pre-Islamic Persian thought; though, owing to our ignorance of the tendencies of Sassanide thought, and of the political, social, and intellectual conditions that determined its evolution, we have not been able fully to trace the continuity of ideas. Nations as well as individuals, in their intellectual history, begin with the objective. Although the moral favour of Zoroaster gave a spiritual tone to his theory of the origin of things, yet the net result of this period of Persian speculation is nothing more than a materialistic dualism. The principle of Unity as a philosophical ground of all that exists, is but dimly perceived at this stage of intellectual evolution in Persia. The controversy among the followers of Zoroaster indicates that the movement towards a monistic conception of the Universe had begun; but we have, unfortunately, no evidence to make a positive statement concerning the pantheistic tendencies of Pre-Islamic Persian thought. We know that in the 6th century A.D., Diogenes, Simplicius and other Neo-

Platonic thinkers were driven by the persecution of Justinian, to take refuge in the court of the tolerant Anūsh̲īrwān. This great monarch, moreover, had several works translated for him from Sanskrit and Greek, but we have no historical evidence to show how far these events actually influenced the course of Persian thought. Let us, therefore, pass on to the advent of Islam in Persia, which completely shattered the old order of things, and brought to the thinking mind the new concept of an uncompromising monotheism as well as the Greek dualism of God and matter, as distinguished from the purely Persian dualism of God and Devil.

PART II
GREEK DUALISM

CHAPTER II

THE NEO-PLATONIC ARISTOTELIANS OF PERSIA

With the Arab conquest of Persia, a new era begins in the history of Persian thought. But the warlike sons of sandy Arabia whose swords terminated, at Nahāwand, the political independence of this ancient people, could hardly touch the intellectual freedom of the converted Zoroastrian.

The political revolution brought about by the Arab conquest marks the beginning of interaction between the Aryan and the Semitic, and we find that the Persian, though he lets the surface of his life become largely semitised, quietly converts Islām to his own Aryan habits of thought. In the West the sober Hellenic intellect interpreted another Semitic religion—Christianity; and the results of interpretation in both cases are strikingly similar. In each case the aim of the interpreting intellect is to soften the extreme rigidity of an absolute law imposed on the individual from without; in one word it is an endeavour to internalise the external. This process of transformation began with the study of Greek thought which, though combined with other causes, hindered the growth of native speculation, yet marked a transition from the purely objective attitude of Pre-Islamic Persian Philosophy to the subjective attitude of later thinkers. It is, I believe, largely due to the influence of foreign thought that the old monistic tendency when it reasserted itself about the end of the 8th century, assumed a much more spiritual aspect ; and, in its latter development, revivified and spiritualised the old Iranian dualism of Light and Darkness. The fact, therefore, that Greek thought roused into fresh life the subtle Persian intellect, and largely contributed to, and was finally assimilated by the general course of intellectual evolution in Persia, justifies us in briefly running over, even though at the risk of repetition, the systems of the Persian Neo-Platonists who, as such, deserve very little attention in a history of purely Persian thought.

It must, however, be remembered that Greek wisdom flowed towards the Moslem east through Harrān and Syria. The Syrians took up the latest Greek speculation i.e. Neo-Platonism and transmitted to the Moslem what they believed to be the real philosophy of Artistotle. It is surprising that Mohammedan Philosophers, Arabs as well as Persians, continued wrangling over what they believed to be the real teaching of Aristotle and Plato, and it never occurred to them that for a thorough comprehension of their Philosophies, the knowledge of Greek language was absolutely necessary. So great was their ignorance that an epitomised translation of the Enneads of Plotinus was accepted as "Theology of Aristotle." It took them centuries to arrive at a clear conception of the two great masters of Greek thought ; and it is doubtful whether they ever completely understood them. Avicenna is certainly clearer and more original than Al-Fārābī and Ibn Maskawaih ; and the Andelusian Averroes, though he is nearer to Aristotle than any of his predecessors, is yet far from a complete grasp of Aristotle's Philosophy. It would, however, be unjust to accuse them of servile imitation. The history of their speculation is one continuous attempt to wade through a hopeless mass of absurdities that careless translators of Greek Philosophy had introduced. They had largely to rethink the Philosophies of Aristotle and Plato. Their commentaries constitute, so to speak, an effort at discovery, not exposition. The very circumstances which left them no time to think out independent systems of thought, point to a subtle mind, unfortunately cabined and cribbed by a heap of obstructing nonsense that patient industry had gradually to eliminate, and thus to window out truth from falsehood. With these preliminary remarks we proceed to consider Persian students of Greek Philosophy individually.

1. IBN MASKAWAIH[1] (d. 1030)

Passing over the names of Sarakhsī[2], Fārābī who

---

[1] Dr. Boer, in his Philosophy of Islām, gives a full account of the Philosophy of Al-Fārābī and Avicenna ; but his account of Ibn Maskawaih's Philosophy is restricted to the Ethical teaching of that Philosopher. I have given here his metaphysical views which are decidedly more systematic than those of Al-Fārābī. Instead of repeating Avicenna's Neo Platonism I have briefly stated what I believe to be his original contribution to the thought of his country.

[2] Sarakhsī died in 899 A.D. He was a disciple of the Arabian Philosopher Al-Kindī. His works, unfortunately, have not reached us.

was a Turk, and the Physician Rāzī (d. 932 A.D.) who true to his Persian habits of thought, looked upon light as the first creation, and admitted the eternity of matter, space and time, we come to the illustrious name of *Abu 'Ali Muhammad ibn Muhammad ibn Ya'qub, commonly known as Ibn Maskawaih* —the treasurer of the Buwaihid Sultan 'Adaduddaula —one of the most *eminent theistic thinkers, physicians, moralists and historians of Persia*. I give below a brief account of his system from his well-known work Al Fauz al-Aṣghar, published in Beirūt.

1. The existence of the ultimate principle

Here Ibn Maskawaih follows Aristotle, and reproduces his argument based on the fact of physical motion. All bodies have the inseparable property of motion which covers all form of change, and does not proceed from the nature of bodies themselves. Motion, therefore, demands an external source of prime mover. The supposition that motion may constitute the very essence of bodies, is contradicted by experience. Man, for instance, has the power of free movement; but, on the supposition, different parts of his body must continue to move even after they are severed from one another. The series of moving causes, therefore, must stop at a cause which, itself immovable, moves everything else. The immobility of the Primal cause is essential; for the supposition of motion in the Primal cause would necessitate infinite regress, which is absurd.

The immovable mover is one. A multiplicity of original movers must imply something common in their nature, so that they might be brought under the same category. It must also imply some point of difference in order to distinguish them from each other. But this partial identity and difference necessitate composition in their respective essences; and composition, being a form of motion, cannot, as we have shown, exist in the first cause of motion. The prime mover again is eternal and immaterial. Since transition from non-existence to existence is a form of motion; and since matter is always subject to some kind of motion, it follows that a thing which is not eternal, or is, in any way, associated with matter, must be in motion.

2. The Knowledge of the Ultimate

All human knowledge begins from sensations which are gradually transformed into perceptions. The earlier stages of intellection are completely conditioned by the presence of external reality. But the progress of knowledge means to be able to think without being conditioned by matter. Thought begins with matter, but its object is to gradually free itself from the primary condition of its own possibility. A higher stage, therefore, is reached in imagination—the power to reproduce and retain in the mind the copy or image of a thing without reference to the external objectivity of the thing itself. In the formation of concepts thought reaches a still higher stage in point of freedom from materiality; though the concept, in so far as it is the result of comparison and assimilation of percepts, cannot be regarded as having completely freed itself from the gross cause of sensations. But the fact that conception is based on perception, should not lead us to ignore the great difference between the nature of the concept and the percept. The individual (percept) is undergoing constant change which affects the character of the knowledge founded on mere perception. The knowledge of individuals, therefore, lacks the element of permanence. The universal (concept), on the other hand, is not affected by the law of change. Individuals change; the universal remains intact. It is the essence of matter to submit to the law of change : the freer a thing is from matter, the less liable it is to change. God, therefore, being absolutely free from matter, is absolutely changeless ; and it is His complete freedom from materiality that makes our conception of Him difficult or impossible. The object of all philosophical training is to develop the power of "ideation" or contemplation on pure concepts, in order that constant practice might make possible the conception of the absolutely immaterial.

3. How the one creates the many

In this connection it is necessary, for the sake of clearness, to divide Ibn Maskawaih's investigations into two parts :—

(a) *That the ultimate agent or cause created the Universe out of nothing.* Materialists, he says, hold the eternity of matter, and attribute form to the creative activity of God. It is, however, admitted that when matter passes from one form into another form, the previous form becomes absolutely non-existent. For if it does not become absolutely non-existent, it must either pass off into some other body, or continue to exist in the same body. The first alternative is contradicted by every-day experience. If we transform a ball of wax into a solid square, the original rotundity of the ball does not pass off into some other body. The second alternative is also impossible ; for it would necessitate the conclusion that two contradictory forms e.g., circularity and length, can exist in the same body. It, therefore, follows that the original form passes into absolute non-existence, when the new form comes into being. This argument proves conclusively that attributes i.e. form, colour etc., come into being from pure nothing. In order to understand that the substance is also non-eternal like the attribute, we should grasp the truth of the following propositions :—

1. The analysis of matter results in a number of different elements, the diversity of which is reduced to one simple element.

2. Form and matter are inseparable : no change in matter can annihilate form.

From these two propositions, Ibn Maskawaih concludes that the substance had a beginning in time. Matter like form must have begun to exist ; since the eternity of matter necessitates the eternity of form which, as we have seen, cannot be regarded as eternal.

(*b*) *The process of creation.* What is the cause of this immense diversity which meets us on all sides? How could the many be created by one? When, says the Philosopher, one cause produces a number of different effects, their multiplicity may depend on any of the following reasons :—

1. The cause may have various powers. Man, for instance, being a combination of various elements and powers, may be the cause of various actions.

2. The cause may use various means to produce a variety of effects.

3. The cause may work upon a variety of material.

None of these propositions can be true of the nature of the ultimate cause—God. That he possesses various powers, distinct from one another, is manifestly absurd; since his nature does not admit of composition. If he is supposed to have employed different means to produce diversity, who is the creator of these means? If these means are due to the creative agency of some cause other than the ultimate cause, there would be a plurality of ultimate causes. If, on the other hand, the Ultimate Cause himself created these means, he must have required other means to create these means. The third proposition is also inadmissible as a conception of the creative act. The many cannot flow from the causal action of one agent. It, therefore, follows that we have only one way out of the difficulty—that the ultimate cause created only one thing which led to the creation of another. Ibn Maskawaih here enumerates the usual Neo-Platonic emanations gradually growing grosser and grosser until we reach the primordial elements, which combine and recombine to evolve higher and higher forms of life. Shiblī thus sums up Ibn Maskawaih's theory of evolution[1] :—

"The combination of primary substances produced the mineral kingdom, the lowest form of life. A higher stage of evolution is reached in the vegetable kingdom. The first to appear is spontaneous grass ; then plants and various kinds of trees, some of which touch the border-land of animal kingdom, in so far as they manifest certain animal characteristics. Intermediary between the vegetable kingdom and the animal kingdom there is a certain form of life which is neither animal nor vegetable, but shares the characteristics of both (e.g., coral). The first step beyond this intermediary stage of life, is the development of the power of movement, and the sense of touch in tiny worms which crawl upon the earth. The sense of touch, owing to the process of differentiation, develops other forms of sense, until we reach the plane of higher animals in which intelligence begins to manifest itself in an ascending scale. Humanity is touched in the ape which undergoes further development, and gradually develops erect stature and power of understanding similar to man. Here animality ends and humanity begins."

4. The Soul

In order to understand whether the soul has an independent existence, we should examine the nature.

[1] Maulānā Shiblī 'Ilm al Kalām, p. 141. (Haidarābād).

of human knowledge. It is the essential property of matter that it cannot assume two different forms simultaneously. To transform a silver spoon into a silver glass, it is necessary that the spoon-form as such should cease to exist. This property is common to all bodies, and a body that lacks it cannot be regarded as a body. Now when we examine the nature of perception, we see that there is a principle in man which, in so far as it is able to know more than one thing at a time, can assume, so to say, many different forms simultaneously. This principle cannot be matter, since it lacks the fundamental property of matter. The essense of the soul consists in the power of perceiving a number of objects at one and the same moment of time. But it may be objected that the soul-principle may be either material in its essence, or a function of matter. There are, however, reasons to show that the soul cannot be a function of matter.

(a) A thing which assumes different forms and states, cannot itself be one of those forms and states. A body which receives different colours should be, in its own nature, colourless. The soul, in its perception of external objects. assumes, as it were, various forms and states ; it, therefore, cannot be regarded as one of those forms. Ibn Maskawaih seems to give no countenance to the contemporary Faculty-Psychology ; to him different mental states are various transformations of the soul itself.

(b) The attributes are constantly changing ; there must be beyond the sphere of change, some permanent substratum which is the foundation of personal identity.

Having shown that the soul cannot be regarded as a function of matter, Ibn Maskawaih proceeds to prove that it is essentially immaterial. Some of his arguments may be noticed :—

1. The senses, after they have perceived a strong stimulus, cannot, for a certain amount of time, perceive a weaker stimulus. It is, however, quite different with the mental act of cognition.

2. When we reflect on an abstruse subject, we endeavour to completely shut our eyes to the objects around us, which we regard as so many hindrances in the way of spiritual activity. If the soul is material in its essence, it need not, in order to secure unimpeded activity, escape from the world of matter.

3. The perception of a strong stimulus weakens and sometimes injures the sense. The intellect, on the other hand, grows in strength with the knowledge of ideas and general notions.

4. Physical weakness due to old age, does not affect mental vigour.

5. The soul can conceive certain propositions which have no connection with the sense-data. The senses, for instance, cannot perceive that two contradictories cannot exist together.

6. There is a certain power in us which rules over physical organs, corrects sense-errors, and unifies all knowledge. This unifying principle which reflects over the material brought before it through the sense-channel, and, weighing the evidence of each sense, decides the character of

rival statements, must itself stand above the sphere of matter.

The combined force of these considerations, says Ibn Maskawaih, conclusively establishes the truth of the proposition—that the soul is essentially immaterial. The immateriality of the soul signifies its immortality; since mortality is a characteristic of the material.

2. AVICENNA (d. 1037)

Among the early Persian Philosophers, Avicenna alone attempted to construct his own system of thought. His work, called "Eastern Philosophy", is still extant; and there has also come down to us a fragment[1] in which the Philosopher has expressed his views on the universal operation of the force of love in nature. It is something like the contour of a system, and it is quite probable that ideas expressed therein were afterwards fully worked out.

Avicenna defines "Love" as the appreciation of Beauty; and from the standpoint of this definition he explains that there are three categories of being:—

1. Things that are at the highest point of perfection.
2. Things that are at the lowest point of perfection.
3. Things that stand between the two poles of perfection. But the third category has no real existence; since there are things that have already

[1] This fragment on love is preserved in the collected works of Avicenna in the British Museum Library and has been edited by N. A. F. Mehren. (Leiden, 1894).

attained the acme of perfection, and there are others still progressing towards perfection. This striving for the ideal is love's movement towards beauty which, according to Avicenna, is identical with perfection. Beneath the visible evolution of forms is the force of love which actualises all striving, movement, progress. Things are so constituted that they hate non-existence, and love the joy of individuality in various forms. The indeterminate matter, dead in itself, assumes, or more properly, is made to assume by the inner force of love, various forms, and rises higher and higher in the scale of beauty. The operation of this ultimate force, in the physical plane, can be thus indicated :—

1. Inanimate objects are combinations of form, matter and quality. Owing to the working of this mysterious power, quality sticks to its subject or substance ; and form embraces indeterminate matter which, impelled by the mighty force of love, rises from form to form.

2. The tendency of the force of love is to centralise itself. In the vegetable kingdom it attains a higher degree of unity or centralisation ; though the soul still lacks that unity of action which it attains afterwards. The processes of the vegetative soul are :—

(*a*) Assimilation.
(*b*) Growth.
(*c*) Reproduction.

These processes, however, are nothing more than so many manifestations of love. Assimilation indicates attraction and transformation of what is external into what is internal. Growth is love of achieving more and more harmony of parts ; and reproduction means perpetuation of the kind, which is only another phase of love.

3. In the animal kingdom, the various operations of the force of love are still more unified. It does preserve the vegetable instinct of acting in different directions ; but there is also the devolpment of temperament which is a step towards more unified activity. In man this tendency towards unification manifests itself in self-consciousness. The same force of "natural or constitutional love," is working in the life of beings higher than man. All things are moving towards the first Beloved— the Eternal Beauty. The worth of a thing is decided by its nearness to, or distance from, this ultimate principle.

As a physician, however, Avicenna is especially interested in the nature of the Soul. In his times, moreover, the doctrine of metempsychosis was getting more and more popular. He, therefore, discusses the nature of the soul, with a view to show the falsity of this doctrine. It is difficult, he says, to define the soul ; since it manifests different powers and tendencies in different planes of being. His view of the various powers of the soul can be thus represented :—

 1. Manifestation as unconscious activity—
  (*a*) Working in different directions (Vegetative soul)   { 1. Assimilation. 2. Growth. 3. Reproduction.
  (*b*) Working in one direction and securing uniformity of action—growth of temperament.

2. Manifestation as conscious activity—
(a) As directed to more than one object—

Animal soul

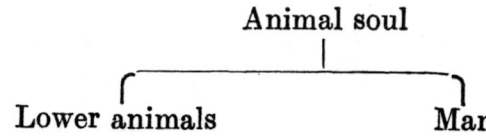

Lower animals

A. Perceptive powers.
B. Motive powers (desire of pleasure and avoidance of pain).

Man

A. Perceptive powers.
  (a) Five external senses.
  (b) Five internal senses—
    1. Sensorium.
    2. Retention of images.
    3. Conception.
    4. Imagination.
    5. Memory.
  These constitute the five internal senses of the soul which, in man, manifests itself as progressive reason, developing from human to angelic and prophetic reason.
B. Motive powers — will.

(b) As directed to one object—The soul of the spheres which continue in one uniform motion.

In his fragment on "Nafs" (soul) Avicenna endeavours to show that a material accompaniment is not necessary to the soul. It is not through the instrumentality of the body, or some power of the body, that the soul conceives or imagines; since if the soul necessarily requires a physical medium in conceiving other things, it must require a different body in order to conceive the body attached to itself. Moreover, the fact that the soul is immediately self conscious—conscious of itself through itself—conclusively shows that in its essence the soul is quite independent of any physical accompaniment. The doctrine of metempsychosis implies, also, individual pre-existence. But supposing that the soul did exist before the body, it must have existed either as one or as many. The multiplicity of bodies is due to the multiplicity of material forms, and does not indicate the multiplicity of souls. On the other hand, if it existed as one, the ignorance or knowledge of A must mean the ignorance or knowledge of B ; since the soul is one in both. These categories, therefore, cannot be applied to the soul. The truth is, says Avicenna, that body and soul are contiguous to each other, but quite opposite in their respective essences. The disintegration of the body does not necessitate the annihilation of the soul. Dissolution or decay is a property of compounds, and not of simple, indivisble, ideal substances. Avicenna, then denies pre-existence, and endeavours to show the possibility of disembodied conscious life beyond the grave.

We have run over the work of the early Persian Neo-Platonists among whom, as we have seen, Avicenna alone learned to think for himself. Of the generations of his disciples—Behmenyār, Ab u'l-Ma'mūm of Isfahān, Ma'ṣumi, Ab u'l-'Abbās, Ibn Tāhir[1]—who carried on their master's Philosophy, we need not speak. So powerful was the spell of Avicenna's personality that, even long after it had been removed, any amplification or modification of his views was considered to be an unpardonable crime. The old Iranian idea of the dualism of Light and Darkness does not act as a determining factor in

---

[1] Al-Baihaqi ; fol. 28a et seqq.

the progress of Neo-Platonic ideas in Persia, which borrowed independent life for a time, and eveutually merged their separate existence in the general current of Persian speculation. They are, therefore, connected with the course of indigenous thought only in so far as they contributed to the strength and expansion of that monistic tendency, which manifested itself early in the Church of Zoroaster ; and, though for a time hindered by the theological controversies of Islām, burst out with redoubled force in later times, to extend its titanic grasp to all the previous intellectual achicvements of the land of its birth.

CHAPTER III

THE RISE AND FALL OF RATIONALISM IN ISLĀM

1. THE METAPHYSICS OF RATIONALISM—MATERIALISM

The Persian mind, having adjusted itself to the new Political environment, soon reasserts its innate freedom, and begins to retire from the field of objectivity, in order that it may come back to itself and reflect upon the material achieved in its journey out of its own inwardness. With the study of Greek thought, the spirit which was almost lost in the concrete, begins to reflect and realise itself as the arbiter of truth. Subjectivity asserts itself, and endeavours to supplant all outward authority. Such a period, in the intellectual history of a people, must be the epoch of rationalism, scepticism, mysticism, heresy—forms in which the human mind, swayed by the growing force of subjectivity, rejects all external standards of truth. And so we find the epoch under consideration.

The period of Umayyad dominance is taken up with the process of co-mingling and adjustment to new conditions of life; but with the rise of the 'Abbāsid Dynasty and the study of Greek Philosophy, the pent-up intellectual force of Persia bursts out again, and exhibits wonderful activity in all the departments of thought and action. The fresh intellectual vigour imparted by the assimilation of Greek Philosophy, which was studied with great avidity, led immediately to a critical examination of Islamic Monotheism. Theology, enlivened by religious fervour, learned to talk the language of Philosophy earlier than cold reason began to seek a retired corner, away from the noise of controversy, in order to construct a consistent theory of things. In the first half of the 8th Century we find Wāsil Ibn 'Atā—a Persian disciple of the famous theologian Hasan of Basra—starting Mu'tazilaism (Rationalism)—that most interesting movement which engaged some of the subtlest minds of Persia, and finally exhausted its force in the keen metaphysical controversies of Baghdad and Basra. The famous city of Basra had become, owing to its commercial situation the play-ground of various forces—Greek Philosophy, Scepticism, Christianity, Buddhistic ideas, Manichaeism[1]—which furnished ample spiritual food to the inquiring mind of the time, and formed the intellectual environment of Islamic Rationalism. What Spitta calls the Syrian period of Muhammadan History is not characterised with metaphysical subtleties. With the advent of the Persian Period, however, Muhammadan students of Greek Philosophy

---

[1] During the 'Abbāsid Period there were many who secretly held Manichaem opinions See Fihrist, Leipzig 1871, p 338; See also Al-Mu'tazila, ed. by T. W. Arnold, Leipzig 1902, p. 27, where the author speaks of a controversy between Abu'l-Hudhail and Sālih, the Dualist. See also Macodonald's Muslim Theology, p. 133.

began properly to reflect on their religion; and the Mu'tazila thinkers[1], gradually drifted into metaphysics with which alone we are concerned here. It is not our object to trace the history of the Mu'tazila Kalām; for present purposes it will be sufficient if we briefly reveal the metaphysical implications of the Mu'tazila view of Islām. The conception of God, and the theory of matter, therefore, are the only aspects of Rationalism which we propose to discuss here.

His conception of the unity of God at which the Mu'tazila eventually arrived by a subtle dialectic is one of the fundamental points in which he differs from the Orthodox Muhammadan. God's attributes, according to his view, cannot be said to inhere in Him; they form the very essence of His nature. The Mu'tazila, therefore, denies the separate reality of divine attributes, and declares their absolute identity with the abstract divine Principle. "God",

[1] The Mu'tzilas belonged to various nationalities, and many of them were Persians either by descent or domicile. Wāsil Ibn 'Atā—the reported founder of the sect—was a Persian (Browne, Lit. His., Vol. 1, p. 281). Von Kremer, however, traces their origin to the theological controversies of the Umayyad period. Mu'tazilaism was not an essentially Persian movement; but it is true, as Prof. Browne observes (Lit. His., Vol. I, p. 283) that Shi'ite and Qādarī tenets, indeed, often went together, and the Shi'ite doctrine current in Persia at the present day is in many respects Mu'tazilite, while Hasan Al-Ash'arī, the great opponent of the Mu'tazilite, is by the Shi'ites held in horror. It may also be added that some of the greater representatives of the Mu'tazila opinion were Shi'as by religion, e.g. Abu'l-Hudhail (Al-Mu'tazila, ed. by T. W. Arnold, p. 281). On the other hand many of the followers of Al-Ash'arī were Persians (See extracts from Ibn 'Asākir ed. Mehren), so that it does not seem to be quite justifiable to describe the Ash'arite mode of thought as a purely Semitic movement.

says Abu'l-Hudhail, "is knowing, all-powerful, living; and His knowledge, power and life constitute His very essence (dhat)"[1]. In order to explain the pure unity of God Joseph Al-Ba.ir[2] lays down the following five principles :—

(1) The necessary supposition of atom and accident.

(2) The necessary supposition of a creator.

(3) The necessary supposition of the conditions (Ahwāl) of God.

(4) The rejection of those attributes which do not befit God.

(5) The unity of God in spite of the plurality of His attributes.

This conception of unity underwent further modifications; until in the hands of Mu'ammar and Abu Hashim it became a mere abstract possibility about which nothing could be predicated. We cannot, he says, predicate knowledge of God[3], for His knowledge must be of something in Himself. The first necessitates the identity of subject and object which is absurd; the second implicates duality in the nature of God which is equally impossible. Ahmad and Fadl[4]—disciples of Nazzām, however, recognised this duality in holding that the original creators are two—God—the eternal principle; and

[1] Shahrastānī : Cureton's ed., p. 34.

[2] Dr. Frankl : Ein Mu'tazilitischer Kalām—Wien 1872, p. 13.

[3] Shahrastānī : Cureton's ed., p. 41. See also Steiner—Die Mutaziliten, p. 59.

[4] Ibn Hazm (Cairo, ed. I) Vol. IV, p. 197. See also Shahrastānī : Cureton's ed., p. 42.

the word of God—Jesus Christ—the contingent principle. But more fully to bring out the element of truth in the second alternative suggested by Mu'ammar, was reserved, as we shall see, for later Sūfi thinkers of Persia. It is, therefore, clear that some of the rationalists almost unconsciously touched the outer fringe of later pantheism for which, in a sense, they prepared the way, not only by their definition of God, but also by their common effort to internalise the rigid externality of absolute law.

But the most important contribution of the advocates of Rationalism to purely metaphysical speculation, is their explanation of matter, which their opponents—the Ash'arite—afterwards modified to fit in with their own views of the nature of God. The interest of Nazzām chiefly consisted in the exclusion of all arbitrariness from the orderly course of nature[1]. The same interest in naturalism led Al-Jāhiz to define Will in a purely negative manner[2]. Though the Rationalist thinkers did not want to abandon the idea of a Personal Will, yet they endeavoured to find a deeper ground for the independence of individual natural phenomena. And this ground they found in matter itself. Nazzām taught the infinite divisibility of matter, and obliterated the distinction between substance and accident[3]. Existence was regarded as a quality super-imposed by God on the pre-existing material atoms which would have been incapable of percep-

---

[1] Steiner ; Die Mu'taziliten ; Leipzig, 1865, p. 57.
[2] Ibid. p. 59.
[3] Shahrastānī ; Cureton's ed., p. 38.

tion without this quality. Muhammad Ibn 'Uthmān, one of the Mu'tazila Shaikhs, says Ibn Hazm[1], maintained that the non-existent (atom in its pre-existential state) is a body in that state; only that in its pre-existential condition it is neither in motion, nor at rest, nor is it said to be created. Substance, then, is a collection of qualities—taste, odour, colour—which, in themselves, are nothing more than material potentialities. The soul, too, is a finer kind of matter; and the processes of knowledge are mere mental motions. Creation is only the actualisation of pre-existing potentialities[2] (Ṭafra). The individuality of a thing which is defined as "that of which something can be predicated"[3] is not an essential factor in its notion. The collection of things we call the Universe, is externalised or perceptible reality which could, so to speak, exist independent of all perceptibility. The object of these metaphysical subtleties is purely theological. God, to the Rationalist, is an absolute unity which can, in no sense, admit of plurality, and could thus exist without the perceptible plurality—the Universe.

The activity of God, then, consists only in making the atom perceptible. The properties of the atom flow from its own nature. A stone thrown up falls down on account of its own indwelling property[4]. God, says Al-'Attār of Baṣra and Bishr ibn

[1] Ibn Ḥazm (ed. Cairo): Vol. V, p. 42.
[2] Shahrastānī: Cureton's ed., p. 38.
[3] Steiner: Die Mu'taziliten, p. 80.
[4] Shahrastānī: Cureton's ed., p. 38.

al-Mu'tamir, did not create colour, length, breadth, taste or smell—all, these are activities of bodies themselves[1]. Even the number of things in the Universe is not known to God[2]. Bi*sh*r ibn al-Mu'tamir further explained the properties of bodies by what he called "Tawallud"—interaction of bodies[3]. Thus it is clear that the Rationalists were philosophically materialists, and theologically deists.

To them substance and atom are identical, and they define substance as a space-filling atom which, besides the quality of filling space, has a certain direction, force and existence forming its very essence as an actuality. In shape it is squarelike; for if it is supposed to be circular, combination of different atoms would not be possible[4]. There is, however, great difference of opinion among the exponents of atomism in regard to the nature of the atom. Some hold that atoms are all similar to each other; while Abu'l-Qāsim of Bal*kh* regards them as similar as well as dissimilar. When we say that two things are similar to each other, we do not necessarily mean that they are similar in all their attributes. Abu'l-Qāsim further differs from Nazzām in advocating the indestructibility of the atom. He holds that the atom had a beginning in time; but that it cannot be completely annihilated. The attribute of "Baqā" (continued exsitence), he says, does not

[4] Ibn Ḥazm (ed. Cairo): Vol. IV, pp. 194, 197.
[9] Ibid. Vol. IV, p. 194.
[4] *Sh*ahrastān: Cureton's ed., p. 44.
[1] In my treatment of the atomism of Islamic Rationalists, I am indebted to Arthur Biram's publication: "Kitābul Masā'il fil *kh*ilāf beyn al-Baṣriyyīn wal Ba*gh*dādiyyīn".

give to its subject a new attribute other than existence; and the continuity of existence is not an additional attribute at all. The divine activity created the atom as well as its continued existence. Abu'l-Qāsim, however, admits that some atoms may not have been created for continued existence. He denies also the existence of any inervening space between different atoms, and holds unlike other representatives of the school, that the essence or atom (Māhiyyat) could not remain essence in a state of non-existence. To advocate the opposite is a contradiction in terms. To say that the essence (which is essence because of the attribute of existence) could remain essence in a state of non-existence, is to say that the existent could remain existent in a state of non-existence. It is obvious that Abu'l-Qāsim here approaches the Ash'arite theory of knowledge which dealt a serious blow to the Rationalist theory of matter.

2. CONTEMPORARY MOVEMENTS OF THOUGHT

Side by side with the development of Mu'tazilaism we see, as is natural in a period of great intellectual activity, many other tendencies of thought manifesting themselves in the philosophical and religious circles of Islam. Let us notice them briefly :—

1. Scepticism. The tendency towards scepticism was the natural consequence of the purely dialectic method of Rationalism. Men such as Ibn Ashras and Al-Jāhiz, who apparently belonged to the Rationalist camp, were really sceptics. The

standpoint of Al-Jāhiz who inclined to deistic naturalism[1], is that of a cultured man of the time, and not of a professional theologian. In him is noticeable also a reaction against the metaphysical hairsplitting of his predecessors, and a desire to widen the pale of theology for the sake of the illiterate who are incapable of reflecting on articles of faith.

2. Sūfiism—an appeal to a higher source of knowledge which was first systematised by Dhu'l-Nūn, and became more and more deepened and antischolastic in contrast to the dry intellectualism of the Ash'arite. We shall consider this interesting movement in the following chapter.

3. The revival of authority—Ismāīlianism—a movement characteristically persian which, instead of repudiating freethought, endeavours to come to an understanding with it. Though this movement seems to have no connection with the theological controversies of the time, yet its connection with freethought is fundamental. The similarity between the methods practised by the Ismāīlian missionaries and those of the partisans of the association called Ikhwān-al-Safā—Brethren of Purity—suggests some sort of secret relation between the two institutions. Whatever may be the motive of those who started this movement, its significance as an intellectual phenomenon should not be lost sight of. The multiplicity of philosophical and religious views — a necessary consequence of speculative activity — is

[1] Macdonald's Muslim Theology, p. 161.

apt to invoke forces which operate against this, religiously speaking, dangerous multiplicity. In the 18th Century history of European thought we see Fichte, starting with a sceptical inquiry concering the nature of matter, and finding its last word in Pantheism. Schleiermacher appeals to Faith as opposed to Reason, Jacobi points to a source of knowledge higher than reason, while Comte abandons all metaphysical inquiry, and limits all knowledge to sensuous perception. De Maistre and Schlegel, on the other hand, find a resting place in the authority of an absolutely infallible Pope. The advocates of the doctrine of Imāmat think in the same strain as De Maistre; but it is curious that the Ismāilians, while making this doctrine the basis of their Church, permitted free play to all sorts of thinking.

The Ismāilia movement then is one aspect of the persistent battle[1] which the intellectually independent Persian waged against the religious and political ideals of Islam. Originally a branch of the Shīite religion, the Ismāilia sect assumed quite a cosmopolitan character with 'Abdulla ibn Maimūn— the probable progenitor of the Fātimid Caliphs of Egypt—who died about the same time when Al-Ashʻarī, the great opponent of Freethought, was born. This curious man imagined a vast scheme in which he weaved together innumerable threads

---

[1] Ibn Ḥazm in his Kitāb al-Milal, looks upon the heretical sects of Persia as a continuous struggle against the Arab power which the cunning Persian attempted to shake off by these peaceful means. See Von Kremer's Geschichte der herrschenden Ideen des Islams, pp. 10, 11, where this learned Arab historian of Cordova is quoted at length.

of various hues, resulting in a cleverly constructed equivocation, charming to the Persian mind for its mysterious character and misty Pythagorean Philosophy. Like the Association of the Brethren of Purity, he made an attempt, under the pious cloak of the doctrine of Imāmat (Authority), to synthesise all the dominating ideas of the time. Greek Philosophy, Christianity, Rationalism, Sūfiism, Manichaeism, Persian heresies, and above all the idea of reincarnation, all came forward to contribute their respective shares to the boldly conceived Ismā'īlian whole, the various aspects of which were to be gradually revealed to the initiated, by the "Leader"—the ever Incarnating Universal Reason—according to the intellectual development of the age in which he incarnated himself. In the Ismā'īlian movement, Freethought, apprehending the collapse of its ever widening structure, seeks to rest upon a stable basis, and, by a strange irony of fate, is led to find it in the very idea which is revolting to its whole being. Barren authority, though still apt to reassert herself at times, adopts this unclaimed child, and thus permits herself to assimilate all knowledge past, present and future.

The unfortunate connection, however, of this movement with the politics of the time, has misled many a scholar. They see in it (Macdonald, for instance) nothing more than a powerful conspiracy to uproot the political power of the Arab from Persia. They have denounced the Ismā'īlian Church which counted among its followers some of the best heads and sincerest hearts, as a mere clique of dark murderers who were ever watching for a possible victim. We must always remember, while estimating the character of these people, the most barbarous persecutions which drove them to pay red-handed fanaticism in the same coin. Assassinations for religious purposes were considered unobjectionable, and even perhaps lawful among the whole Semite race. As late as the latter half of the 16th Century, the Pope of Rome could approve such a dreadful slaughter as the massacre of St. Bartholomew. That assassination, even though actuated by religious zeal, is still a crime, is a purely modern idea; and justice demands that we should not judge older generations with our own standards of right and wrong. A great religious movement which shook to its very foundations the structure of a vast empire, and, having successfully passed through the varied ordeals of moral reproach, calumny and persecution, stood up for centuries as a champion of Science and Philosophy, could not have entirely rested on the frail basis of a political conspiracy of a mere local and temporary character. Ismā'īlianism, in spite of its almost entire loss of original vitality, still dominates the ethical ideal of not an insignificant number in India, Persia, Central Asia, Syria and Africa; while the last expression of Persian thought—Bābism is essentially Ismā'īlian in its character.

To return, however, to the Philosophy of the sect. From the later Rationalists they borrowed their conception of Divinity. God, or the ultimate principle of existence, they teach, has no attribute. His nature admits of no predication When we predicate the attribute of power to Him, we only mean that He is the giver of power; when we predicate eternity, we indicate the eternity of what the Qur'ān calls "Amr" (word of God) as distinguished from the "Khalq" (creation of God) which is contingent. In His nature all contradictions melt away, and from Him flow all opposites. Thus they considered themselves to have solved the problem which had troubled the mind of Zoroaster and his followers.

In order to find an answer to the question, "What is plurality?" the Ismā'īlia refer to what they consider a metaphysical axiom—"that from one only one can proceed". But the one which proceeds is not something completely different from which it proceeds. It is really the Primal one transformed. The Primal Unity, therefore, transformed itself into the First Intellect (Universal Reason); and then, by means of this transformation of itself, created the Universal soul which, impelled by its nature to perfectly identify itself with the original source, felt the necessity of motion, and consequently of a body possessing the power of motion. In order to achieve its end, the soul created the heavens moving in circular motion according to its direction. It also created the elements which mixed together, and formed the visible Universe—the scene of plurality through which it endeavours to pass with a view to come back to the original source. The individual soul is an epitome of the whole Universe which exists only for its progressive education. The Universal Reason incarnates itself from time to time, in the personality of the "Leader" who illuminates the soul in proportion to its experience and understanding, and gradually guides it through the scene of plurality to the world of eternal unity. When the Universal soul reaches its goal, or rather returns to its own deep being, the process of disintegration ensues. "Particles constituting the Universe fall off from each other—those of goodness go to truth (God) which symbolises unity; those of evil go to untruth (Devil) which symbolises diversity"[1]. This is but briefly the Ismā'īlian Philosophy—a mixture, as Sharastānī remarks, of Philosophical and Manichaean ideas—which, by gradually arousing the slumbering spirits of scepticism, they administered, as it were, in doses to the initiated, and finally brought them to that stage of spiritual emancipation where solemn ritual drops off, and dogmatic religion appears to be nothing more than a systematic arrangement of useful falsehoods.

The Ismā'īlian doctrine is the first attempt to amalgamate contemporary Philosophy with a really Persian view of the Universe, and to restate Islām, in reference to this synthesis, by allegorical interpretation of the Qur'ān—a method which was afterwards adopted by Ṣūfīism. With them the Zoroastrian Ahriman (Devil) is not the malignant creator of evil things but it is a principle which violates the eternal unity, and breaks it up into visible diversity. The

[1] Sharastānī : Cureton's ed : p. 149.

idea that some principle of difference in the nature of the ultimate existence must be postulated in order to account for empirical diversity, underwent further modifications; until in the Ḥurūfī sect (an offshoot of the Ismāʻīlia), in the 14th Century, it touched contemporary Ṣufīism on the one hand, and Chiristian Trinity onthe other. The "Be", maintained the Ḥurūfīs, is the eternal word of God, which, itself uncreated, leads to further creation—the word externalised. "But for the 'word' the recognition of the essence of Divinity would have been impossible; since Divinity is beyond the reach of sense—perception"[1]. The 'word', therefore, became flesh in the womb of Mary[2] in order to manifest the Father. The whole Universe is the manifestation of God's 'word', in which He is immanent[3]. Every sound in the Universe is within God; every atom is singing the song of eternity[4]; all is life. Those who want to discover the ultimate reality of things, let them seek "the named" through the Name[5], which at once conceals and reveals its subject.

3. REACTION AGAINST RATIONALISM THE ASH'ARITE

Patronised by the early Caliphs of the House of ʻAbbās, Rationalism continued to flourish in the intellectual centres of the Islamic world; until, in the first half of the 9th Century, it met the powerful

[1] Jāwidān Kabīr, fol. 149a.
[2] Ibid. fol. 280a.
[3] Ibid. fol. 366b.
[4] Ibid. fol. 155b.
[5] Ibid. fol. 382a.

orthodox reaction which found a very energetic leader in Al-Ash'arī (b. 873 A.D.) who studied under Rationalist teachers only to demolish, by their own methods, the edifice they had so laboriously built. He was a pupil of Al-Jubbā'ī[1] — the representative of the younger school of Mu'tazilaism in Baṣra — with whom he had many controversies[2] which eventually terminated their friendly relations, and led the pupil to bid farewell to the Mu'tazila camp. "The fact", says Spitta, "that Al-Ash'arī was so thoroughly a child of his time with the successive currents of which he let himself go, makes him, in another relation, an important figure to us. In him, as in any other, are clearly reflected the various tendencies of this politically as well as religiously interesting period; and we seldom find ourselves in a position to weigh the power of the orthodox confession and the Mu'tazilite speculation, the child-like helpless manner of the one, the immaturity and imperfection of the other, so completely as in the life of this man who was orthodox as a boy and a Mu'tazila as a young man"[3]. The Mu'tazila speculation (e. g. Al-Jāḥiz) tended to be absolutely unfettered, and in some cases led to a merely negative attitude of thought. The movement initiated by Al-Ash'arī was an attempt not only to purge Islām of all non-Islamic

---

[1] Extracts from Ibn 'Asākir (Mehren)—Travaux de la troisiéme session du Congrés International des Orientalistes— p. 261.

[2] Spitta: Zur Geschichte Abul-Hasan Al-Ash'arī, pp. 42, 43. See also Ibn Khallikān (Gottingen 1839)—Al-Jubbā'ī, where the story of their controversy is given.

[3] Spitta: Vorwort, p. VII.

elements which had quietly crept into it, but also to harmonize the religious consciousness with the religious thought of Islam. Rationalism was an attempt to measure reality by reason alone; it implied the identity of the spheres of religion and philosophy, and strove to express faith in the form of concepts or terms of pure thought. It ignored the facts of human nature, and tended to disintegrate the solidarity of the Islamic Church. Hence the reaction.

The orthodox reaction led by the Ash'arite then was, in reality, nothing more than the transfer of dialectic method to the defence of the authority of Divine Revelation. In opposition to the Rationalists, they maintained the doctrine of the Attributes of God; and, as regards the Free Will controversy, they adopted a course lying midway between the extreme fatalism of the old school, and the extreme libertarainism of the Rationalists. They teach that the power of choice as well as all human actions are created by God; and that man has been given the power of acquiring[1] the different modes of activity. But Fakhral-Din Razi, who in his violent attack on philosophy was strenuously opposed by Tusi and Qutbal-Din does away with the idea of "acquisition", and openly maintains the doctrine of necessity in his commentary on the Qur'ān. The Mātrīdiyya—another school of anti-rationalist theology, founded by Abu Mansūr Mātarīdī a native of Mātarīd in the environs of Samarqand—went back to the old

[1] Sharastānī—ed. Cureton, p. 69.

rationalist position, and taught in opposition to the Ash'arite, that man has absolute control over his activity ; and that his power affects the very nature of his actions. Al-Ash'arī's interest was purely theological ; but it was impossible to harmonise reason and revelation without making reference to the ultimate nature of reality. Bāqilānī[1], therefore, made use of some purely metaphysical propositions (that substance is an individual unity ; that quality cannot exist in quality ; that perfect vacuum is possible) in his theological investigation, and thus gave the school a metaphysical foundation which it is our main object to bring out. We shall not, therefore, dwell upon their defence of orthodox beliefs (e.g., that the Qur'ān is uncreated ; that the visibility of God is possible etc.) ; but we shall endeavour to pick up the elements of metaphysical thought in their theological controversies. In order to meet contemporary philosophers on their own ground, they could not dispense with philosophising ; hence willingly or unwilling they had to develop a theory of knowledge peculiar to themselves.

God, according to the Ash'arite, is the ultimate necessary existence which "carries its attributes in its own being"[2]; and whose existence (wujūd) and essence (Māhiyyat) are identical. Besides the argument from the contingent character of motion they

[2] Martin Schreiner : Zur Geschichte dez Ash'aritenthums. (Huitiéme Congréss International des Orientalistes 1889, p. 82).
[2] Martin Schreiner ; Zur Geschichte des As'aritenthums. (Huitiéme Congrés International des Orientalistes IIme Partie 1893, p. 113).

used the following arguments to prove the existence of this ultimate principle :—

(1) All bodies, they argue, are one in so far as the phenomenal fact of their existence is concerned. But in spite of this unity, their qualities are different and even opposed to each other. We are, therefore, driven to postulate an ultimate cause in order to account for their empirical divergence.

(2) Every contingent being needs a cause to account for its existence. The universe is contingent; therefore it must have a cause; and that cause is God. That the Universe is contingent, they proved in the following manner. All that exists in the Universe is either substance or quality. The contingence of quality is evident, and the contingence of substance follows from the fact that no substance could exist apart from qualities. The contingence of quality necessitates the contingence of substance; otherwise the eternity of substance would necessitate the eternity of quality. In order fully to appreciate the value of this argument, it is necessary to understand the Ash'arite theory of knowledge. To answer the question, "What is a thing?" they subjected to a searching criticism the Aristotelian categories of thought, and arrived at the conclusion that bodies have no properties in themselves[1]. They made no distinction of secondary and primary qualities of a body, and reduced all of them to purely subjective relations. Quality too

[1] See Macdonald's admirable account of The Ash'arite Metaphysics : Muslim Theology p. 201 sq. See also Maulānā Shiblī, 'Ilmal Kalām pp. 60, 72.

became with them a mere accident without which the substance could not exist. They used the word substance or atom with a vague implication of externality; but their criticism, actuated by a pious desire to defend the idea of divine creation, reduced the Universe to a mere show of ordered subjectivities which, as they maintained like Berkeley, found their ultimate explanation in the Will of God. In his examination of human knowledge regarded as a product and not merely a process, Kant stopped at the idea of "Ding an sich", but the Ash'arite endeavoured to penetrate further, and maintained, against the contemporary Agnostic-Realism, that the so-called underlying essence existed only in so far as it was brought in relation to the knowing subject. Their atomism, therefore, approaches that of Lotze[1] who, in spite of his desire to save external reality, ended in its complete reduction to ideality. But like Lotze they could not believe their atoms to be the inner working of the Infinite Primal Being. The interest of pure monotheism was too strong for them. The necessary consequence of their analysis of matter is a thorough going idealism like that of Berkeley; but perhaps their instinctive realism combined with the force of atomistic tradition, still compels them to use

[1] "Lotze is an atomist, but he does not conceive the atoms themselves as material; for extension, like all other sensuous qualities is explained through the reciprocal action of atoms; they themselves, therefore, cannot possess this quality. Like life and like all empirical qualities, the sensuous fact of extension is due to the co-operation of points of force, which, in time, must be conceived as starting points of the inner working of the Infinite Primal Being". Höffding Vol. II, p. 516.

the word "atom" by which they endeavour to give something like a realistic colouring to their idealism. The interest of dogmatic theology drove them to maintain towards pure Philosophy an attitude of criticism which taught her unwilling advocates how to philosophise and build a metaphysics of their own.

But a more important and philosophically more significant aspect of the Ash'arite Metaphysics, is their attitude towards the Law of Causation[1]. Just as they repudiated all the principles of optics[2] in order to show, in opposition to the Rationalists, that God could be visible in spite of His being unextended, so with a view to defend the possibility of miracles, they rejected the idea of causation altogether. The orthodox believed in miracles as well as in the Universal Law of Causation; but they maintained that, at the time of manifesting a miracle, God suspended the operation of this law. The Ash'arite, however, starting with the supposition that cause and effect must be similar, could not share the orthodox view, and taught that the idea of power is meaningless, and that we know nothing but floating impressions, the phenomenal order of which is determined by God.

Any account of the Ash'arite metaphysics would be incomplete without a notice of the work of Al-Ghazāli (d. 1111 A.D.) who though misunderstood by many orthodox theologians, will always be looked

[1] Shibli 'Ilmal-Kalām, pp. 64, 72.
[2] Shahrastāni, ed. Cureton, p. 82.

upon as one of the greatest personalities of Islām. This sceptic of powerful ability anticipated Descartes[1] in his philosophical method ; and, " seven hundred years before Hume cut the bond of causality with the edge of his dialectic"[2]. He was the first to write a systematic refutation of philosophy, and completely to annihilate that dread of intellectualism which had characterised the orthodox. It was chiefly his influence that made men study dogma and metaphysics together, and eventually led to a system of education which produced such men as Shahrastānī, Al-Rāzī and Al-Ishrāqī. The following passage indicates his attitude as a thinker :—

"From my childhood I was inclined to think out things for myself. The result of this attitude was that I revolted against authority ; and all the beliefs that had fixed themselves in my mind from childhood lost their original importance. I thought that such beliefs based on mere authority were equally entertained by Jews, Christians, and followers of other religions. Real knowledge must eradicate all doubt. For instance, it is self-evident that ten is greater than three. If a person, however, endeavours to prove the contrary by an appeal to his power of turning a stick into a snake, the performance would indeed be wonderful, though it cannot touch the

---

[1] "It (Al-Ghazālī's work on the Revivication of the sciences of religion) has so remarkable a resemblance to the *Discourse sur la methode* of Descartes, that had any translation of it existed in the days of Descartes everyone would have cried against the plagiarism." (Lewes's History of Philosophy : Vol. II. p. 50).

[2] Journal of the American Oriental Society, Vol. 20, p. 103.

certainty of the proposition in question"[1]. He examined afterwards, all the various claimants of "Certain Knowledge" and finally found it in Sūfīism.

With their view of the nature of substance, the Ash'arite, rigid monotheists as they were, could not safely discuss the nature of the human soul. Al-Ghazālī alone seriously took up the problem, and to this day it is difficult to define, with accuracy, his view of the nature of God. In him, like Borger and Solger in Germany, Sūfī pantheism and the Ash'arite dogma of personality appear to harmonise together, a reconciliation which makes it difficult to say whether he was a Pantheist, or a Personal Pantheist of the type of Lotze. The soul, according to Al-Ghazālī, perceives things. But perception as an attribute can exist only in a substance or essence which is absolutely free from all the attributes of body. In his Al-Madnūn[2], he explains why the Prophet declined to reveal the natrue of the soul. There are, he says, two kinds of men; ordinary men and thinkers. The former, who look upon materiality as a condition of existence, cannot conceive an immaterial substance. The latter are led, by their logic, to a conception of the soul which sweeps away all difference between God and the individual soul. Al-Ghazālī, therefore, realised the Pantheistic drift of his own inquiry, and preferred silence as to the ultimate nature of the soul.

[1] Al-Munqidh, p. 3.
[2] See Sir Sayyid Ahmad's criticism of Al-Ghazālī's view of the soul, Al-Nazrufī ba'di Masāili-l Imāmi-l humām Abu Hāmid Al-Ghazālī; No. 4, p. 3 sq. (ed. Agra).

He is generally included among the Ash'arite. But strictly speaking he is not an Ash'arite; though he admitted that the Ash'arite mode of thought was excellent for the masses. "He held", says Shiblī ('Ilmal-Kalām, p. 66), "that the secret of faith could not be revealed; for this reason he encouraged exposition of the Ash'arite theology, and took good care in persuading his immediate disciples not to publish the results of his private reflection". Such an attitude towards the Ash'arite theology, combined with his constant use of philosophical language, could not but lead to suspicion. Ibn Jauzī, Qāḍī 'Iyāḍ, and other famous theologians of the orthodox school, publicly denounced him as one of the "misguided"; and 'Iyāḍ went even so far as to order the destruction of all his philosophical and theological writings that existed in Spain.

It is, therefore, clear that while the dialectic of Rationalism destroyed the personality of God, and reduced divinity to a bare indefinable universality, the antirationalist movement, though it preserved the dogma of personality, destroyed the external reality of nature. In spite of Nazzām's theory of "Atomic objectification"[1], the atom of the Rationalist possesses an independent objective reality; that of the Ash'arite is a fleeting moment of Divine Will. The one saves nature, and tends to do away with the God of Theology; the other sacrifices nature to save God as conceived by the orthodox.

[1] Ibn Hazm, Vol. V, pp. 63, 64, where the author states and criticises this theory.

The God-intoxicated Ṣūfī who stands aloof from the theological controversies of the age, saves and spiritualises both the aspects of existence, and looks upon the whole Universe as the self-revelation of God—a higher notion which synthesises the opposite extremes of his predecessors. "Wooden-legged" Rationalism, as the Ṣūfī called it, speaks its last word in the sceptic Al-Ghazālī, whose restless soul, after long and hopeless wanderings in the desolate sands of dry intellectualism, found its final halting place in the still deep of human emotion. His scepticism is directed more to substantiate the necessity of a higher source of knowledge than merely to defend the dogma of Islamic Theology, and, therefore, marks the quiet victory of Ṣūfīism over all the rival speculative tendencies of the time.

Al-Ghazālī's positive contribution to the Philosophy of his country, however, is found in his little book—Mishkātal-Anwār—where he starts with the Qurānic verse, "God is the light of heavens and earth", and instinctively returns to the Iranian idea, which was soon to find a vigorous expounder in Al-Ishrāqī. Light, he teaches in this book, is the only real existence; and there is no darkness greater than non-existence. But the essence of Light is manifestation: "it is attributed to manifestation which is a relation"[1]. The Universe was created out of darkness on which God sprinkled[2] his own

[1] Mishkātal-Anwār, fol. 3a.
[2] In support of this view Al-Ghazālī quotes a tradition of the Prophet. Ibid. fol. 10a.

light, and made its different parts more or less visible according as they received more or less light. As bodies differ from one another in being dark, obscure, illuminated or illuminating, so men are differentiated from one another. There are some who illuminate other human beings; and, for this reason, the Prophet is named "The Burning Lamp" in the Qur'ān.

The physical eye sees only the external manifestation of the Absolute or Real Light. There is an internal eye in the heart of man which, unlike the physical eye, sees itself as other things, an eye which goes beyond the finite, and pierces the veil of manifestation. These thoughts are merely germs, which developed and fructified in Al-Ishrāqī's "Philosophy of Illumination"—Ḥikmatal-Ishrāq.

Such is the Ash'arite Philosophy.

One great theological result of this reaction was that, it checked the growth of freethought which tended to dissolve the solidarity of the Church. We are, however, concerned more with the purely intellectual results of the Ash'arite mode of thought, and these are mainly two:—

(1) It led to an independent criticism of Greek Philosophy as we shall see presently.

(2) In the beginning of the 10th Century, when the Ash'arite had almost completely demolished the stronghold of Rationalism, we see a tendency towards what may be called Persian Positivism.

Al-Birūnī[1] (d. 1048) and Ibn Haitham[2] (d. 1038) who anticipated modern empirical Psychology in recognising what is called reaction-time, gave up all inquiry concerning the nature of the supersensual, and maintained a prudent silence about religious matters. Such a state of things could have existed, but could not have been logically justified before Al-Ash‘arī.

[1] He (Al-Birūnī) quotes with approval the following, as the teaching of the adherents of Aryabhatta ; It is enough for us to know that which is lighted up by the sun's rays. Whatever lies beyond, though it should be of immeasurable extent, we cannot make use of ; for what the sunbeam does not reach, the senses do not perceive, and what the senses do not perceive we cannot know. From this we gather what Al-Birūnī's Philosophy was : only sense-perceptions, knit together by a logical intelligence, yield sure knowledge. (Boer's Philosophy in Islām, p. 146).

[2] "Moreover truth for him (Ibn Haitham) was only that which was presented as material for the faculties of sense-perception, and which received it from the understanding, being thus the logically elaborated perception". (Boer's Philosophy in Islām, p. 150).

CHAPTER IV

CONTROVERSY BETWEEN IDEALISM AND REALISM

The Ash'arite denial of Aristotle's Prima Materia, and their views concerning the nature of space, time and causation, awakened that irrepressible spirit of controversy which, for countries, divided the camp of Muhammedan thinkers, and eventually exhausted its vigor in the merely verbal subtleties of schools. The publication of Najim al Dīn Al-Kātibī's (a follower of Aristotle whose disciples were called Philosophers as distinguished from scholastic theologians) Ḥikmat al-'Ain—"Philosophy of Essence", greatly intensified the intellectual conflict, and invoked keen criticism from a host of Ash'arite as well as other idealist thinkers. I shall consider in order the principle points on which the two schools differed from each other.

A. The Nature of the Essence

We have seen that the Aṣl'arite theory of knowledge drove them to hold that individual essences of various things are quite different from each other, and are determined in each case by the ultimate cause—God. They denied the existance of an ever-changing primary stuff common to all things, and maintained against the Rationalists that existence constitutes the very being of the essence.

To them, therefore, essence and existence are identical. They argued that the Judgment, "Man is animal", is possible only on the ground of a fundamental difference between the subject and the predicate ; since their identity would make the Judgment nugatory, and complete difference would make the predication false. It is, therefore, necessary to postulate an external cause to determine the various forms of existence. Their opponents, however, admit the determination or limitation of existence, but they maintain that all the various forms of existence, in so far as their essence is concerned, are identical—all being limitations of one Primary substance. The followers of Aristotle met the difficulty suggested by the possibility of synthetic predication, by advocating the possibility of compound essences. Such a judgment as "Man is animal", they maintained, is true ; because man is an essence composed of two essences, animility and humanity. This, retorted the Ash'arite, cannot stand criticism. If you say that the essence of man and animal is the same, you in other words hold that the essence of the whole is the same as that of the part. But this proposition is absurd ; since if the essence of the compound is the same as that of its constituents, the compound will have to be regarded as one being having two essences or existences.

It is obvious that the whole controversy turns on the question whether existence is a mere idia or something objectively real. When we say that a certain thing exists, do we mean that it exists only in relation to us (Ash'arite position) ; or that it is an essence existing quite independently of us (Realist position) ? We shal briefly indicate the arguments of either side. The Realist argued as follows :—

(1) The conception of my existence is something immediate or intuitive. The thought "I exist" is a "concept", and my body being an element of this "concept", it follows that my body intuitively known as something real. If the knowledge of the existent is not immediate, the fact of its perception would require a process of thought which, as we know, it does not. The Ash'arite Al-Rāzī admits that the concept of existence is immediate ; but he regards the judgment— "The concept of existence is immediate" — as merely a matter of acquisition. Muḥammad Ibn Mubārak Bukhārī on the other hand, says that the whole argument of the realist proceeds on the assumption that the concept of my existance is something immediate—a position which can be controverted.[1] If, says he, we admit that the concept of my existence is immediate, abstract existence cannot be regarded as a constitutive element of this conception. And if the realist maintains that the perception of a particular object is immediate, we admit the truth of what he says ; but it would not follow, as he is anxious to establish, that the so-called underlying essence is immediately known as objectively real. The realist argument, moreover, demands that the mind ought not to be able to conceive the predication of qualities to

[1] Muḥammad ibn Mubārak's Commentary on Ḥikmat al-'Ain, fol. 5a.

things. We cannot conceive, "snow is white", because whiteness, being a part of this immediate judgment, must also be immediately known without any predication. Mulla Muḥammad Hāshim Husainī remarks[1] that this reasoning is erroneous. The mind in the act of predicating whiteness of snow is working on a purely ideal existence—the quality of whiteness—and not on an objectively real essence of which the qualities are mere facets or espects. Ḥusainī, moreover, anticipates Hamilton, and differs from other realist in holding that the so-called unknownable essence af the object is also immediately known. The object, he says, is immediately perceived as one.[2] We do not successively perceivo the various aspects of what happens to be the objects of our perception.

(2) The idealist, says the realist, reduces all quality to mere subjective relations. His argument leads him to deny the underlying essence of things, and to look upon them as entirely heterogeneous collections of qualities, the essence of which consists merely in the phenomenal fact of their perception. Iu spite of his belief in the complete heterogeneity of things, he applies the word existence to all things— a tacit admission that there is some essence common to all the various forms of existence. Abu'l-Ḥasan al-Ashʿarī replies that this application is only a verbal convenience, and is not meant to indicate the so-called internal homogeneity of things. But the

---

[1] Husainī's Commentary on Ḥikmat al-ʿAin, fol. 13a.
[2] Ibid. fol. 14b.

universal application of the word existence by the idealists, must mean, according to the realist, that the existence of a thing either constitutes its very essence, or it is something superadded to the underlying essence of the thing. The first supposition is a virtual admission as to the homogeneity of things; since we cannot maintain that existence peculiar to one thing is fundamentally different from existence peculiar to another. The supposition that existence is something superadded to the essence of a thing leads to an absurdity; since in this case the essence will have to be regarded as something distinct from existence; and the denial of essence (with the Ash'arite) would blot out the distinction between existence and non-existence. Moreover, what was the essence before existence was superadded to it? We must not say that the essence was ready to receive existence before it actually did receive it; since this statement would imply that the essence was non-existence before it received existence. Likewise the statement that the essence has the power of receiving the quality of non-existence, implies the absurdity that it does already exist. Existence, there-fore, must be regarded as forming a part of the essence. But if it forms a part of the essence, the latter will have to be regarded as a compound. If, on the other hand, existence is external to the essence, it must be something contingent because of its dependence on something other than itself. Now eveything contingent must have a cause. If this cause is the essence itself, it would follow that the essence existed before it existed; since the cause must precede the effect in the fact of existence. If, however, the cause of existence is something other than the essence, it follows that the existence of God also must be explained by some cause other than the essence of God—an absurd conclusion which turns the necessary into the contingent.[1] This argument of the realist is based on a complete misunderstanding of the idealist position. He does not see that the idealist never regarded the fact of existence as something superadded to the essence of a thing; but always held it to be identical with the essence. The essence, says ibn Mubārak,[2] is the cause of existence without being chronologically before it. The existence of the essence constitutes its very being; it is not dependent for it on something other than itself.

The truth is that both sides are far from a true theory of knowledge. The agnostic realist who holds that behind the phenomenal qualities of a thing, there is an essence operating as their cause, is guilty of a glaring contradiction. He holds that underlying the thing there is an *unknowable* essence or substratum which is *known* to exist. The Ash'arite idealist, on the other hand, misunderstands the process of knowledge. He ignores the mental activity involved in the act of knowledge; and looks upon perceptions as mere presentations which are determined, as he says, by God. But if the order of presentations requires a cause to account for it, why should not that cause be sought in the original

---

[1] Ibn Mubārak's Commentary, fol. 8b.
[2] Ibid, fol. 9a.

constitution of matter as Locke did? Moreover, the theory that knowledge is a mere passive perception or awareness of what is presented, leads to certain inadmissible conclusions which the Ash'arite never thought of:—

(a) They did not see that their purely subjective conception of knowledge swept away all possibility of error. If the existence of a thing is merely the fact of its being presented, there is no reason why it should be cognised as different from what it actually is.

(b) They did not see that on their theory of knowledge, our fellow-beings, like other elemets of the physical order, would have no higher reality than mere states of my consciousness.

(c) If knowledge is a mere receptivity of presentations, God, who, as cause of presentations, is active in regard to the act of our knowledge, must not be aware of our presentations. From the Ash'arite point of view this conclusion is fatal to their whole position. They cannot say that presentations, on their ceasing to be my presentations, continue to be presentations to God's consciousness.

Another question connected with the nature of the essence is, whether it is caused or uncaused. The followers of Aristotle, or philosophers as they are gonerally called by their opponents, hold that the underlying essence of things is uncaused. The Ash'arite hold the opposite view. Essence, says the Aristotelian, cannot be acted upon by any external agent.[1] Al-Kātibī argues that if, for instance, the

[1] Ibn Mubārak's Commentary, fol. 20a.

essence of humanity had resulted from the operation of an external activity, doubt as to its being the real essence of humanity would have been possible. As a matter of fact we never entertain such a doubt; it follows therefore, that the essence is not due to the activity of an agency external to itself. The idealist starts with the realist distinction of essence and existence, and argues that the realist line of argument would lead to the absurd proposition — that man is uncaused; since he must be regarded, according to the realist, as a combination of two uncaused essences—existence and humanity.

B. The Nature of Knowledge

The followers of Aristotle, true to their position as to the independent objective reality of the essence, define knowledge as "receiving images of external things".[1] It is possible to conceive, they argue, an object which is externally unreal, and to which other qualities can be attributed. But when we attribute to it the quality of existence, actual existence is necessitated ; since the affirmation of the quality of a thing is a part of the affirmation of that thing. If, therefore, the predication of existence does not necessitate actual objective existence of the thing, we are driven to deny externality altogether, and to hold that the thing exists in the mind as a mere idea. But the affirmation of a thing, says Ibn Mubarak, constitutes the very existence of the thing. The idealist makes no such distinction as affirmation and existence. To infer from the above argument that

[1] Ibn Mubārak. fol. 11a.

the thing must be regarded as existing in the mind, is unjustifiable. "Ideal" existence follows only from the denial of externality which the Ash'arite do not deny; since they hold that knowledge is a relation between the knower and the known which is known as external. Al-Kātibī's proposition that if the thing does not exist as external existence, it must exist as ideal or mental existence, is self-contradictory; since, on his principles, everything that exists in idea exists in externality.[1]

C. The Nature of Non-existence

Al-Kātibī explains and criticises the proposition, maintained by contemporary philosophers generally —"That the existent is good, and the non-existent is evil"[2]. The fact of murder, he says, is not evil because the murderer had the power of committing such a thing; or because the instrument of murder had the power of cutting; or because the neck of the murdered had the capacity of being cut asunder. It is evil because it signifies the negation of life— a condition which is non-existential, and not existential like the conditions indicated above. But in order to show that evil is non-existence, we should make an inductive inquiry, and examine all the various cases of evil. A perfect induction, however, is impossible, and an incomplete induction cannot prove the point. Al-Kātibī, therefore, rejects this proposition, and holds that "non-existence is abso-

---

[1] Ibn-Mubārak. fol. 11b.
[2] Ibid. fol. 4a.

lute nothing"[1]. The possible *'essences'*, according to him, are not lying fixed in space waiting for the attribute of existence; otherwise fixity in space would have to be regarded as possessing no existence. But his critics hold that this argument is true only on the supposition that fixity in space and existence are identical. Fixity in externality, says Ibn Mubārak, is a conception wider than existence. All existence is external, but all that is external is not necessarily existent.

The interest of the Ash'arite in the dogma of the Ressurrection—the possibility of the reappearance of the non-existent as existent—led them to advocate the apparently absurd proposition that "non—existence or nothing *is* something". They argued that, since we make judgments about the non-existent, it is, therefore, known; and the fact of its knowability indicates that "the nothing" is not absolutely nothing. The knowable is a case of affirmation and the non-existent being knowable, is a case of affirmation.[2] Al-Kātibī denies the truth of the Major. Impossible things, he says, are known, yet they do not externally exist. Al-Rāzī criticises this argument accusing Al-Kātibī of the ignorance of the fact that the *'essence'* exists in the mind, and yet is known as external. Al-Kātibī supposes that the knowledge of a thing necessitates its existence as an independent objective reality. Moreover it should be remembered that the Ash'arite discriminate between positive and existent

---

[1] Ibn Mubārak's Commentary, fol. 14b.
[2] Ibn Mubārak's Commentary, fol. 15a.

on the one hand, and non-existent and negative on the other. They say that all existent is positive, but the converse of this proposition is not true. There is certainly a relation between the existent and the non-existent, but there is absolutely no relation between the positive and the negative. We do not say, as Al-Kātibī holds, that the impossible is non-existent; we say that the impossible is only negative. Substances which do exist are something positive. As regards the attribute which cannot be conceived as existing apart from the substance, it is neither existent nor nonexistent, but something between the two. Briefly the Ash'arite position is as follows:—

"A thing has a proof of its existence or not. If not, it is called negative. If it has a proof of its existence, it is either substance or attribute. If it is substance and has the attribute of existence or non-existence (i.e. it is perceived or not) it is existent or non-existent accordingly. If it is attribute, it is neither existent nor non-existent".[1]

[1] Ibn Mubārak's Commentary, fol. 15b.

CHAPTER V
SUFIISM

I. THE ORIGIN AND QURANIC JUSTIFICATION OF SUFIISM

It has become quite a fashion with modern oriental scholarship to trace the chain of influences. Such a procedure has certainly great historical value, provided it does not make us ignore the fundamental fact, that the human mind possessee an independent individuality, and, acting on its own initiative, can gradually evolve out of itself, truths which may have been anticipated by other minds ages ago. No idea can seize a people's soul unless, in some sense, it is the people's own. External influences may wake it up from its deep unconscious slumber; but they cannot so to speak, create it out of nothing.

Much has been written about the origin of Persian Sūfīism; and, in almost all cases, explorers of this most interesting field of research have exercised their ingenuity in discovering the various channels through which the basic ideas of Sūfīism might have travelled from one place to another. They seem completely to have ignoreed the principle, that the full significance of a phenomenon in the intellectual evolution of a people, can only be comprehended in the light of those pre- existing intellectual, political, and social conditions which alone make its existence inevitable. Von Kremer and Dozy derive Persian Ṣūfīism from the Indian Vedanta; Merx and Mr. Nicholson derive it from Neo-Platonism; while Professor Browne once regarded it as Aryan reaction against an unemotional Semitic religion. It appears to me, however, that these theories have been worked out under the influence of a notion of causation which is essentially false. That a fixed qantity A is the cause of, or produces another fixed quantity B, is a proposition which, though convenient for scientific purposes, is apt to damage all inquiry, in so far as it leads us completely to ignore the innumerable conditions lying at the back of a phenomenon. It would, for instance, be an historidal error to say that the dissolution of the Roman Empire was due to the barbarian invasions. The statement completely ignores other forces of a different character that tended to split up the political unity of the Empire. To describe the advent of barbarian invasions as the cause of the dissolution of the Roman Empire which could have assimilated, as it actually did to a certain extent, the so-called cause, is a procedure that no logic would justify. Let us, therefore, in the light of a truer theory of causaion, enumerate the principal political, social, and intellectual conditions of Islamic life about the end of the 8th and the first half of the 9th Century when, properly speaking, the Ṣūfī ideal of life came into existence, to be soon followed by a philosophical justification of that ideal.—

(1) When we study the history of the time, we find it to be a time of more or less political unrest.

The latter half of the 8th Century presents, besides the political revolution which resulted in the overthrow of the Umayyads (749 A.D), persecutions of Zendiks, and revolts of Persian heretics (Sindbāh 755-6; Ustādhīs 766-8; the veiled prophet of Khurāsān 777-80) who, working on the credulity of the people, cloaked, like Lamennais in our own times, political projects under the guise of religious ideas. Later on in the beginning of the 9th Century we find the sons of Hārūn (Ma'mūn and Amīn) engaged in a terrible conflict for political supremacy ; and still later, we see the Golden Age of Islamic literature seriously disturbed by the persistent revolt of the Mazdakite Bābak (816-838). The early years of Ma'mūn's reign present another social phenomenon of great political significance—the Shu'ūbiyya controversy (815), which progresses with the rise and establishment of independent Persian families, the Tāhirīd (820), the Saffārīd (868), and the Sāmānīd Dynasty (874). It is, therefore, the combined force of these and other conditions of a similar nature that contributed to drive away spirits of devotional character from the scene of continual unrest to the blissful peace of an ever- deepening contemplative life. The Semitic character of the life and thought of these early Muhammadan ascetics is gradually followed by a large hearted pantheism of a more or less Aryan stamp, the development of which, in fact, runs parallel to the slowly progressing political independence of Persia.

(2) *The sceptical tendencies of Islamic Rationalism*

which found an early expression in the poems of Bashshār ibn Burd — the blind Persian sceptic who deified fire, and scoffed at all non-persian modes of thought. The germs of Scepticism latent in Rationalism ultimately necessitated an appeal to a super-intellectual source of knowledge which asserted itself in the Risāla of Al-Qushairī (986). In our own times the negative results of Kant's Critique of PureReason drove Jacobi and Schleiermacher to base faith on the feeling of the reality of the ideal; and to the 19th Century sceptic Wordsworth uncovered that mysterious state of mind "in which we grow all spirit and see into the life of things".

(3) The unemotional piety of the various schools of Islam—the Hanafite (Abu Hanīfa d. 767), the Shāfiite (Al-Shafi'ī d. 820), the Mālikite (Al-Mālik d. 795), and the anthropomorphic Hambalite (Ibn Hambal d. 855)—the bitterest enemy of independent thought—which ruled the masses after the death of Al-Mā'mūn.

(4) The religious discussions among the representatives of various creeds encouraged by Al-Māmūn, and especially the bitter theological controversy between the Ash'arites and the advocates of Rationalism which tended not only to confine religion within the narrow limits of schools, but also stirred up the spirit to rise above all petty sectarian wrangling.

(5) The gradual softening of religious fervency due to the rationalistic tendency of the early Abbāsid period, and the rapid growth of wealth which

tended to produce moral laxity and indifference to religious life in the upper circles of Islām.

(6) The presence of Christianity as a working ideal of life. It was, however, principally the actual life of the Christian hermit rather than his religious ideas, that exercised the greatest fascination over the minds of early Islamic saints whose complete unworldliness, though extremely charming in itself, is, I believe, quite contrary to the spirit of Islam.

Such was principally the environment of Ṣūfiism, and it is to the combined action of the above conditions that we should look for the origin and development of Sūfīistic ideas. Given these conditions and the Persian mind with an almost innate tendency towards monism, the whole phenomenon of the birth and growth of Ṣūfīism is explained. If we now study the principal pre-existing conditions of Neo-Platonism, we find that similar conditions produced similar results. The barbarian raids which were soon to reduce Emperors of the Palace to Emperors of the Camp, assumed a more serious aspect about the middle of the Third Century. Plotinus himself speaks of the political unrest of his time in one of his letters to Flaccus.[1] When he looked round himself in Alexandria, his birthplace, he noticed signs of growing toleration and indifferentism towards religious life. Later on in Rome

[1] "Tidings have reached us that Valerian has been defeated, and is now in the hands of Sapor. The threats of Franks and Allemanni, of Goths and Persians, are alike terrible by turns to our *degenerate* Rome." (Plotinus to Flaccus; quoted by Vaughan in his Half-hours with Mystics, p. 63)

which had become, so to say, a pantheon of different nations, he found a similar want of seriousness in life, a similar laxity of character in the upper classes of society. In more learned circles philosophy was studied as a branch of literature rather than for its own sake; and Sextus Empiricus, provoked by Antiochus's tendency to fuse scepticism and Stoicism was teaching the old unmixed scepticism Pyrrho—that intellectual despair which drove Plotinus to find truth in a revelation above thought itself. Above all, the hard unsentimental character of Stoic morality, and the loving piety of the followers of Christ who, undaunted by long and fierce persecutions, were preaching the message of peace and love to the whole Roman world, necessitated a restatement of pagan thought in a way that might revivify the older ideals of life, and suit the new spiritual requirements of the people. But the ethical force of Christianity was too great for Neo-Platonism which, on account of its more metaphysical[1] character, had no message for the people at large, and was consequently inaccessible to the rude barbarian who, being influenced by the actual life of the persecuted Christian adopted Christianity, and settled down to construct new empires out of the ruins of the old. In Persia the influence of culture-

---

[1] The element of ecstacy which could have appealed to some minds was thrown into the background by the later teachers of Neo Platonism, so that it became a mere system of thought having no human interest. Says Whittaker: "The mystical ecstacy was not found by the later teachers of the school easier to attain, but more difficult; and the tendency became more and more to regard it all but unattainable on earth." Neo-Platonism. p. 101.

contacts and cross-fertilisation of ideas created in certain minds a vague desire to realise a similar restatement of Islām, which gradually assimilated Christian ideas as well as Christian Gnostic speculation, and found a firm foundation in the Qur'ān. The flower of Greek Thought faded away before the breath of Christianity; but the burning simoom of Ibn Taimiyya's invective could not touch the freshness of the Persian rose. The one was completaly swept away by the flood of barbarian invasions; the other, unaffected by the Tartar revolution, still holds its own.

This extraordinary vitality of the Ṣūfī restatement of Islām, however, is explained when we reflect on the all-embracing structure of Ṣūfīism. The Semitic formula of salvation can be briefly stated in the words, "Transform your will"—which signifies that the Semite looks upon will as the essence of the human soul. The Indian Vedantist, on the other hand, teaches that all pain is due to our mistaken attitude towards the Universe. He, therefore, commands us to transform our understanding—implying thereby that the essential nature of man consists in thought, not activity or will. But the Ṣūfī holds that the mere transformation of will or understanding will not bring peace; we should bring about the transformation of both by a complete transformation of feeling, of which will and understanding are only specialised forms. His message to the individual is—" Love all, and forget your own individuality in doing good to others." Says Rūmī: " To win other people's hearts is the greatest pilgrimage; and one heart is worth more than a thousand Ka'bāhs. Ka'bah is a mere cottage of Abraham; but the heart is the very home of God." But this formula demands a *why* and a *how*—a metaphysical justification of the ideal in order to satisfy the understanding; and rules of action in order to guide the will. Ṣūfīism furnishes both. Semitic religion is a code of strict rules of conduct; the Indian Vedanta, on the other hand, is a cold system of thought. Ṣūfīism avoids their incomplete psychology, and attempts to synthesise both the Semitic and the Aryan formulas in the higher category of Love. On the one hand it assimilates the Buddhistic idea of Nirvāna (Fanā— Annihilation), and seeks to build a metaphysical system in the light of this idea; on the other hand it does not disconnect itself from Islām, and finds the justification of its view of the Universe in the Qur'ān. Like the geographical position of its home, it stands midway between the Semitic and the Aryan; assimilating ideas from both sides, and giving them the stamp of its own individuality which, on the whole, is more Aryan than Semitic in character. It would, therefore, be evident that the secret of the vitality of Ṣūfīism is the complete view of human nature upon which it is based. It has survived orthodox persecutions and political revolutions, because it appeals to human nature in its entirety; and, while it concentrates its interest chiefly in a *life* of self-denial, it allows free play to the speculative tendency as well.

I will now briefly indicate how Ṣūfī writers justify their views from the Qurānic standpoint. There is no historical evidence to show that the Prophet of Arabia actually communicated certain esoteric doctrines to 'Alī or Abū Bakr. The Ṣūfī, however, contends that the Prophet had an esoteric teaching—" wisdom "—as distinguished from the teaching contained in the Book, and he brings forward the following verse to substantiate his case : " As we have sent a prophet to you from among yourselves who reads our verses to you, purifies you, teaches you the Book and the *Wisdom*, and teaches you *what you did not know before.*"[1] He holds that "the wisdom" spoken of in the verse, is something not incorporated in the teaching of the Book which, as the Prophet repeatedly declared, had been taught by several prophets before him. If, he says, the wisdom is included in the Book, the word " Wisdom " in the verse would be redundant. It can, I think, be easily shown that in the Qur'ān, as well as in the authenticated traditions, there are germs of Ṣūfī doctrine which, owing to the thoroughly practical genius of the Arabs, could not develop and fructify in Arabia, but which grew up into a distinct doctrine when they found favourable circumstances in alien soils. The Qur'ān thus defines the Muslims : " Those who believe in the Unseen, establish daily prayer, and spend out of what We have given them."[2] But the question arises as to the *what* and the *where* of the

[1] Sura 2 : v. 146.
[2] Sura 2 : v. 2.

Unseen. The Qur'ān replies that the Unseen is in your own soul—" And in the earth there are signs to those who believe, and in yourself,—what! do you not then see!"[1] And again—" We are nigher to him (man) than his own jugular vein."[2] Similarly the Holy Book teaches that the essential nature of the Unseen is pure light—" God is the light of heavens and earth."[3] As regards the question whether this Primal Light is personal, the Qur'ān, in spite of many expressions signifying personality, declares in a few words—" There is nothing like him."[4]

These are some of the chief verses out of which the various Ṣūfī commentators develop pantheistic views of the Universe. They enumerate the following four stages of spiritual training through which the soul—the order or reason of the Primal Light—(" Say that the soul is the order or reason of God."[5]) has to pass, if it desires to rise above the common herd, and realise its union or identity with the ultimate source of all things:—

(1) Belief in the Unseen.

(2) Search after the Unseen. The spirit of inquiry leaves its slumber by observing the marvellous phenomena of nature. " Look at the camel how it is created; the skies how they are exalted; the mountains how tley are unshakeably fixed."[6]

[1] Sura 51 : v. 20, 21.
[2] Sura 50 : v. 15.
[3] Sura 24 : v. 35..
[4] Sura 42 : v. 9.
[5] Sura 17 : v. 87.
[6] Sura 88 : v. 20.

(3) The knowledge of the Unseen. This comes, as we have indicated above, by looking into the depths of our own soul.

(4) The Realisation. This results, according to the higher Ṣūfīism from the constant practice of Justice and Charity—" Verily God bids you do justice and good, and give to kindred (their due), and He forbids you to sin, and do wrong, and oppress".[1]

It must, however, be remembered that some later Sūfī fraternities (e.g. Naqshbandī) devised, or rather borrowed[2] from the Indian Vedantist, other means of bringing about this Realisation. They taught, imitating the Hindu doctrine of Kundalinī, that there are six great centres of light of various colours in the body of man. It is the object of the Ṣūfī to make them move, or to use the technical word, "current", by certain methods of meditation, and eventually to realise, amidst the apparent diversity of colours, the fundamental colourless light which makes everything visible, and is itself invisible. The continual movement of these centres of light through the body, and the final realisation of their identity, which results from putting the atoms of the body into definite courses of motion by slow repetition of the

---

[1] Sura 16 : v. 92.

[2] Weber makes the following statement on the authority of Lassen :—" Al-Birūnī translated Patanjali's work into Arabic at the beginning of the 11th Century, and also, it would appear, the Sānkhya sūtra, though the information we have as to the contents of these works does not harmonise with the Sanskrit originals." History of Indian Literature, p 239.

various names of God and other mysterious expressions, illuminates the whole body of the Ṣūfī; and the perception of the same illumination in the external world completely extinguishes the sense of "otherness". The fact that these methods were known to the Persian Ṣūfīs misled Von Kremer, who ascribed the whole phenomenon of Ṣūfīism to the influence of Vedantic ideas. Such methods of contemplation are quite un-Islamic in character, and the higher Ṣūfīs do not attach any importance to them.

2. ASPECTS OF SUFI METAPHYSICS

Let us now return to the various schools, or rather the various aspects, of Ṣūfī Metaphysics. A carful investigation of Ṣūfī literatnre shows that Ṣūfīism has looked at the Ultimate Reality from three standpoints which, in fact, do not exclude but complement each other. Some Ṣūfīs conceive the essential nature of reality as self-conscious will, others beauty, others again hold that Reality is essentially Thought, Light or Knowledge. There are, therefore, three aspects of Ṣūfī thought :—

A. Reality as Self-conscious Will

The first in historical order is that represented by Shaqiq Balkhi, Ibrahim Adham, Rābi‘a, and others. This school conceives the Ultimate Reality as "Will", and the Universe a finite activity of that will. It is essentially monotheistic and consequently more Semitic in character. It is not the desire of knowledge which dominates the ideal of the Ṣūfīs of this school, but the characteristic features of their life are piety, unworldiness, and an intense longing for God due to the consciousness of sin. Their object is not to philosophise, but principally to work out a certain ideal of life. From our standpoint, therefore, they are not of much importance.

B. Reality as Beauty

In the beginning of the 9th Century Ma'rūf Karkhī defined Ṣūfīism as "Apprehension of Divine realities"[1]—a definition which marks the movement from Faith to Knowledge. But the method of apprehending the ultimate reality was formally stated by Al-Qushairī about the end of the 10th Century. The teachers of this school adopted the Neo-Platonic idea of creation by intermediary agencies; and though this idea lingered in the minds of Ṣūfī writers for a long time, yet their Pantheism led them to abandon the Emanation theory altogether. Like Avicenna they looked upon the Ultimate Reality as "Eternal Beauty", whose very nature consists in seeing its own "face" reflected in the Universe-mirror. The Universe, therefore, became to them a reflected image of the "Eternal Beauty", and not an emanation as the Neo-Platonists had taught. The cause of creation, says Mīr Sayyid Sharīf, is the manifestation of Beauty,

[1] Mr. Nicholson has collected the various definitions of Ṣūfīism. See J. R. A. S. April, 1906.

and the first creation is Love. The realisation of this Beauty is brought by universal love, which the innate Zoroastrian instinct of the Persian Ṣūfī loved to define as "the Sacred Fire which burns up everything other than God", Says Rūmī :

> "O thou pleasant madness, Love !
> Thou Physician of all our ills !
> Thou healer of pride,
> Thou Plato and Galen of our souls !"[1]

As a direct consequence of such a view of the Universe, we have the idea of impersonal absorption which first appears in Bāyazīd of Bistām, and which constitutes the characteristic feature of the later development of this school. The growth of this idea may have been influenced by Hindu pilgrims travelling through Persia to the Buddhistic temple still existing at Bāku.[2] The school became wildly pantheistic in Husain Manṣūr who, in the true spirit of the Indian Vedantist, cried out, "I am God"—Aham Brahma asmi.

---

[1] Mathnavī, Jalāl al Dīn Rūmī, with Bahral 'ulūm's Commentary. Lucknow (India) 1877, p. 9.

[2] As regards the progress of Buddhism, Geiger says :— " We know that in the period after Alexander, Buddhism was powerful in Eastern Iran, and that it counted its confessors as far as Tabaristan. It is especially certain that many Buddhistic priests were found in Bactria. This state of things, which began perhaps in the 1st Century before Christ, lasted till the 7th Century A. D., when the appearance of Islamism alone cut short the development of Buddhism in Kabul and Bactria, and it is in that period that we will have to place the rise of the Zarathushtra legend in the form in which it is presented to us by Daqīqī."
Civilisation of Eastern Iranians
Vol. II, p. 170.

The Ultimate Reality or Eternal Beauty, according to the Ṣūfīs of this school, is infinite in the sense that "it is absolutely free from the limitations of beginning, end, right, left, above, and below."[1] The distinction of essence and attribute does not exist in the Infinite—"Substance and quality are really identical."[2] We have indicated above that nature is the mirror of the Absolute Existence. But according of Nasafī, there are two kinds of mirrors[3]—

(a) That which shows merely a reflected image—this is external nature.

(b) That which shows the real essence—this is man who is a limitation of the Absolute, and erroneously thinks himself to be an independent entity.

"O Derwish!" says Nasafī, "dost thou think that thy existence is independent of God? This is a great error."[4] Nasafī explains his meaning by a beautiful parable.[5] The fishes in a certain tank realised that they lived, moved, and had their being in water, but felt that they were quite ignorant of the real nature of what constituted the very source of their life. They resorted to a wiser fish in a great river, and the philosopher-fish addressed them thus:—

"O you who endeavour to unite the knot (of being)! You are born in union, yet die in the thought of an unreal separation. Thirsty on the

---
[1] Nasafī's Maqṣdai Aqṣā : fol. 8b.
[2] Ibid. fol. 10b.
[3] Ibid. fol. 23b.
[4] Ibid. fol. 3b.
[5] Ibid. fol. 15b.

sea-shore ! Dying penniless while master of the treasure !"

All feeling of separation, therefore, is ignorance ; and all "otherness" is a mere appearance, a dream, a shadow—a differentiation born of relation essential to the self-recognition of the Absolute. The great prophet of this school is "the excellent Rūmī", as Hegel calls him. He took up the old Neo-Platonic idea of the Universal Soul working through the various spheres of being, and expressed it in a way so modern in spirit that Clodd introduces the passage in his "Story of Creation".. I venture to quote this famous passage in order to show how successfully the poet anticipates the modern concept of evolution, which he regarded as the realistic side of his Idealism.

> First man appeared in the class of inorganic things,
> Next he passed therefrom into that of plants.
> For years he lived as one of the plants,
> Remembering nought of his inorganic state so different ;
> And when he passed from the vegetive to the animal state,
> He had no remembrance of his state as a plant,
> Except the inclination he felt to the world of plants,
> Especially at the time of spring and sweet flowers ;
> Like the inclination of infants towards their mothers,
> Which know not the cause of their inclination to the breast.
> Again the great Creator as you know,
> Drew man out of the animal into the human state.
> Thus man passed from one order of nature to another,
> Till he became wise and knowing and strong as he is now.
> Of his first soul he has now no remembrance,
> And he will be again changed from his present soul.
> (Mathnavī : Book IV).

It would now be instructive if we compare this

aspect of Ṣūfī thought with the fundamental ideas of Neo-Platonism. The God of Neo-Platonism is immanent as well as transcendant, "As being the cause of all things, it is everywhere. As being other than all things, it is nowhere. If it were only 'everywhere', and not also 'nowhere', it would *be* all things."[1] The Ṣūfī, however, tersely says that God *is* all things. The Neo-Platonist allows a certain permanence or fixity to matter[2]; but the Ṣūfīs of the school in question regard all empirical experience as a kind of dreaming. Life in limitation, they say, is asleep; death brings the awakening. It is, however, the doctrine of Impersonal Immortality—"genuinely Eastern in spirit"—which distinguishes this school from Neo-Platonism. "Its (Arabian Philosophy) distinctive doctrine", says Whittaker, "of an Impersonal immortality of the general human intellect is, however, as contrasted with Aristotelianism and Neo-Platonism, essentially original."

The above brief exposition shows that there are three basic ideas of this mode of thought:

(*a*) That the Ultimate Reality is knowable through a supersensual state of consciousness;

(*b*) That the Ultimate Reality is impersonal;

(*c*) That the Ultimate Reality is one.

Corresponding to these ideas we have:

(*a*) The Agnostic reaction as manifested in the poet 'Umar Khayyām (12th Century) who cried out

---

[1] Whittaker's Neo-Platonism p. 58.
[2] Whittaker's Neo-Platonism, p. 57.

in his intellectual despair :—

> The joyous souls who quaff potations deep,
> And saints who in the mosque sad vigils keep,
> Are lost at sea alike, and find no shore,
> One only wakes, all others are asleep.

(*b*) The monotheistic reaction of Ibn Taimiyya and his followers in the 13th Century.

(*c*) The Pluralistic reaction of Wāhid Mahmud [1] in the 13th Century.

Speaking from a purely philosophical standpoint, the last movement is most interesting. The history of Thought illustrates the operation of certain general laws of progress which are true of the intellectual annals of different people. The German systems of monistic thought invoked the pluralism of Herbart; while the pantheism of Spinoza called forth the monadism of Leibniz. The operation of the same law led Wāhid Mahmud to deny the truth of contemporary monism, and declare that Reality is not one, but many. Long before Leibniz he taught that the Universe is a combination of what he called "Afrād"—essential units, or simple atoms which have existed from all eternity, and are endowed with life. The law of the Universe is an ascending perfection of elemental matter, continually passing from lower to higher forms determined by the kind of food which the fundamental units assimilate. Each period of his cosmogony comprises 8,000 years, and after eight such periods the world is decomposed,

[1] Dabistān, Chap. 8.

and the units re-combine to construct a new universe. Wāḥid Maḥmūd succeeded in founding a sect which was cruelly persecuted, and finally stamped out of existence by Shāh 'Abbās. It is said that the poet Ḥāfiz of Shīrāz believe in the tenets of this sect.

C. **Reality as Light or Thought**

The third great school of Ṣūfiism conceives Reality as essentially Light or Thought, the very nature of which demands something to be thought or illuminated. While the preceding school abandoned Neo-Platonism, this school transformed it into new systems. There are, however, two aspects of the metaphysics of this school. The one is genuinely Persian in spirit, other is chiefly influenced by Christian modes of thought. Both agree in holding that the fact of empirical diversity necessitates a principle of difference in the nature of the Ultimate Reality. I now proceed to consider them in their historical order.

1. REALITY AS LIGHT—AL-ISHRAQI

Return to Persian Dualism

The application of Greek dialectic to Islamic Theology around that spirit of critical examination which began with Al-Ash'arī, and found its completest expression in the scepticism of Al-Ghazāli. Even among the Rationalists there were some more critical minds—such as Nazzām—whose attitude towards Greek Philosophy was not one of servile submission but of independent criticism. The defenders of dogma—Al-Ghazālī, Al-Rāzī, Abul Barakāt, and Āl-Amidī, carried on a persistent attack on the whole fabric of Greek Philosophy; while Abu Sa'īd Ṣairāfī, Qāḍī 'Abdal Jabbār, Abul Ma'ālī, Abul Qāsim, and finally the acute Ibn Taimiyya, actuated by similar theological motives, continued to expose the inherent weakness of Greek Logic. In their criticism of Greek Philosophy, these thinkers were supplemented by some of the more learned Ṣūfīs, such as Shahābal Dīn Suhrawardī, who endeavoured to substantiate the helplessness of pure reason by his refutation of Greek thought in a work entitled "The Unveiling of Greek Absurdities". The Ash'arite reaction against Rationalism resulted not only in the development of a system of metaphysics most modern in some of its aspects, but also in completely breaking asunder the worn out fetters of intellectual thraldom. Erdmann [1] seems to think that the speculative spirit among the Muslims exhausted itself with Al-Fārābī and Avicenna, and that after them Philosophy became bankrupt in passing over into scepticism and mysticism. Evidently he ignores the Muslim criticism of Greek Philosophy which led to the Ash'arite Idealism on the one hand, and a genuine Persian reconstruction on the other. That a system of thoroughly Persian character might be possible, the destruction of foreign thought, or rather the weakening of its hold on the mind, was

[1] Vol. I, p. 367.

indispensable. The Ash'arite and other defenders of Islamic Dogma completed the destruction; Al-Ishrāqī —the child of emancipation—came forward to build a new edifice of thought; though, in his process of reconstruction, he did not entirely repudiate the older material. His is the genuine Persian brain which, undaunted by the threats of narrow-minded authority, asserts its right of free independent speculation. In his philosophy the old Iranian tradition, which had found only a partial expression in the writings of the physician Al-Rāzī, Al-Ghazālī, and the Ismā'īlia sect, endeavours to come to a final understanding with the philosophy of his predecessors and the theology of Islam.

Shaikh Shahābal Dīn Suhrawardī, known as Shaikhal Ishrāq Maqtūl was born about the middle of the 12th Century. He studied philosophy with Majd Jīlī—the teacher of the commentator Al-Rāzī —and, while still a youth, stood unrivalled as a thinker in the whole Islamic world. His great admirer Al-Malik-al-Zāhir— the son of Sultan Salā-Salāh-al Dīn—invited him to Aleppo, where the youthful philosopher expounded his independent opinions in a way that aroused the bitter jealousy of contemporary theologians. These hired slaves of bloodthirsty Dogmatism, which, conscious of its inherent weakness, has always managed to keep brute force behind its back, wrote to Sultan Salāh-al Dīn, that the Shaikh's teaching was a danger to Islām, and that it was necessary, in the interest of the Faith, to nip the evil in the bud. The Sultan consented; and there, at the early age of 36, the young Persian thinker calmly met the blow which made him a martyr of truth, and immortalised his name for ever. Murderers have passed away, but the philosophy, the price of which was paid in blood, still lives, and attracts many an earnest seeker after truth.

The principal features of the founder of the Ishrāqī Philosophy are his intellectual independence, the skill with which he weaves his materials into a systematic whole, and above all his faithfulness to the philosophic traditions of his country. In many fundamental points he differs from Plato, and freely criticises Aristotle whose philosophy he looks upon as a mere preparation for his own system of thought, Nothing escapes his criticism. Even the logic of Aristotle he subjects to a searching examination, and shows the hollowness of some of its doctrines. Definition, for instance, is genus plus differentia, according to Aristotle. But Al-Ishrāqī holds that the distinctive attribute of the thing defined, which cannot be predicated of any other thing, will bring us no knowledge of the thing. We define "horse" as a neighing animal. Now we understand animality, because we know many animals in which this attribute exists; but it is impossible to understand the attribute "neighing", since it is found nowhere except in the thing defined. The ordinary definition of horse, therefore, would be meaningless to a man who has never seen a horse. Aristotelian definition, as a scientific principle is quite useless. This criticism leads the Shaikh to a standpoint very similar to that of Bosanquet who defines definition, as "Summation of qualities". The Shaikh holds that a true definition would enumerate all the essential attributes which, taken collectively, exist nowhere except in the thing defined, though they may individually exist in other things.

But let us turn to his system of metaphysics, and estimate the worth of his contribution to the thought of his country. In order fully to comprehend the purely intellectual side of Transcendental Philosophy, the student, says the Shaikh, must be thoroughly acquainted with Aristotelian Philosophy, Logic, Mathematics, and Ṣūfīism. His mind should be completely free from the taint of prejudice and sin, so that he may gradually develop that inner sense, which verifies and corrects what intellect understands only as theory. Unaided reason is untrustworthy; it must always be supplemented by "Dhauq"—the mysterious perception of the essence of things—which brings knowledge and peace to the restless soul, and disarms Scepticism for ever. We are, however, concerned with the purely speculative side of this spiritual experience—the results of the inner perception as formulated and systematised by discursive thought. Let us, therefore, examine the various aspects of the Ishrāqī Philosophy—Ontology, Cosmology, and Psychology.

Ontology

The ultimate principle of all existence is "Nūr-i-Qāhir"—the Primal Absolute Light whose essential nature consists in perpetual illumination. "Nothing is more visible than light, and visibility does not stand in need of any definition."[1] The essence of Light, therefore, is manifestation. For if manifestation is an attribute superadded to light, it would follow that in itself light possesses no visibility, and becomes visible only through something else visible in itself; and from this again follows the absurd consequence, that something other than light is more visible than light The Primal Light, therefore, has no reason of its existence beyond itself. All that is other than this original principle is dependent, contingent, possible. The "not-light" (darkness) is not something distinct proceeding from an independent source. It is an error of the representatives of the Magian religion to suppose that Light and Darkness are two distinct realities created by two distinct creative agencies. The ancient philosopheres of Persia were not dualists like the Zoroastrian priests who, on the ground of the principle that the one cannot cause to emanate from itself more than one, assigned two independent sources to Light and Darkness. The relation between them is not that of contrariety; but of existence and non-existence. The affirmation of Light necessarily posits its own negation — Darkness, which it must illuminate in order to be itself. This Primordial Light is the source of all motion. But its motion is not change of place; it is due to the *love* of illumination which constitutes its very essence, and stirs it up, as it were, to quicken all things into life, by

[1] Sharh Awāriyya—Al-Harawī's Commentary on Al-Ishrāqī's Hikmat al-Ishrāq, fol. 10a.

pouring out its own rays into their being. The number of illuminations which proceed from it is infinite. Illuminations of intenser brightness become, in their turn, the sources of other illuminations; and the scale of brightness gradually descends to illumina tions too faint to beget other illuminations. All these illuminations are mediums, or in the language of Theology, angels through whom the infinite varieties of being receive life and sustenance from the Primal Light. The followers of Aristotle erroneously restricted the number of original Intellects to ten. They likewise erred in enumerating the categories of thought. The possibilities of the Primal Light are infinite ; and the Universe, with all its variety, is only a partial expression of the infinitude behind it. The categories of Aristotle, therefore, are only relatively true. It is impossible for human thought to comprehend, within its tiny grasp, all the infinite variety of ideas acording to which the Primal Light does or may illuminate that which is not light. We can, however, discriminate between the following two illuminations of the original Light:—

(1) The Abstract Light (e.g, Intellect, Universal well as individual). It has no form, and never becomes the attribute of anything other than itself (Substance). From it proceed all the vorious forms of partly-conscious, conscious, or self-conscious light, differing from one another in the amount of lustre, which is determined by their comparative

nearness or distance from the ultimate source of their being. The individual intellect or soul is only a fainter copy, or a more distant reflection of the Primal Light. The Abstract Light knows itself through itself, and does not stand in need of a non-ego to reveal its own existence to itself. Consciousness or self-knowledge, therefore, is the very essence of Abstract light, as distinguished from the negation of light.

(2) The Accidental light (Attribute)—the light that has a form, and is capable of becoming an attribute of something other than itself (e.g., the light of the stars, or the visibility of other bodies). The Accidental light, or more properly sensible light, is a distant reflection of the Abstract light, which, because of its distance, has lost the intensity, or substance-character of its parent. The process of continuous reflection is really a softening process; successive illuminations gradually lose their intensity until, in the chain of reflections, we reach certain less intense illuminations which entirely lose their independent character, and cannot exist except in association with something else. These illuminations form the Accidental light—the attribute which has no independent existence. The relation, therefore, between the Accidental and the Abstract light is that of cause and effect. The effect, however, is not something quite distinct from its cause; it is a transformation, or a weaker form of the supposed cause itself. Anything other than the Abstract light (e.g., the nature of the illuminated body itself) cannot be the cause of the

Accidental light; since the latter, being merely contingent and consequently capable of being negatived, can be taken away from bodies without affecting their character. If the essence, or nature of the illuminated body, had been the cause of the Accidental light, such a process of disillumination could not have been possible. We cannot conceive an inactive cause.[1]

It is now obvious that Shaikh al-Ishrāq agree with the Ash'arite thinkers in holding that there is no such thing as the Prima Materia of Aristotle; though he recognises the existence of a necessary; negation of Light—Darkness, the object of illumination. He further agrees with them in teaching the relativity of all categories except Substance and Quality. But he corrects their theory of knowledge, in so far as he recognises an active element in human knowledge. Our relation with the object of our knowledge is not merely a passive relation; the individual soul, being itself an illumination, illuminates the object in the act of knowledge. The Universe to him is one great process of active illumination; but, from a purely intellectual standpoint, this illumination is only a partial expression of the infinitude of the Primal Light, which may illuminate according to other laws not known to us. The categories of thought are infinite; our intellect works with a few only. The shaikh, therefore, from the standpoint of discursive thought, is not far from modern Humanism.

[1] Sh. An : fol. 11 b.

Cosmology

All that is "not-light" is, what the Ishrāqī thinkers call, "Absolute quantity", or "Absolute matter". It is only another aspect of the affirmation of light, and not an independent principle, as the followers of Aristotle erroneously hold. The experimental fact of the transformation of the primary elements into one another points to this fundamental Absolute matter which, with its various degrees of grossness, constitutes the various spheres of material being. The absolute ground of all things, then, is divided into two kinds :—

(1) That which is beyond space—the obscure substance or atoms (essences of the Ash'arite).

(2) That which is necessarily in space—forms of darkness, e.g., weight, smell, taste, etc.

The combination of these two particularises the Absolute matter. A material body is forms of darkness plus obscure substance, made visible or illuminated by the Abstract light. But what is the cause of the various forms of darkness ? These, like the forms of light, owe their existence to the Abstract light, the different illuminations of which cause diversity in the spheres of being. The forms, which make bodies differ from one another, do not exist in the nature of the Absolute matter. The Absolute quantity and the Absolute matter being identical, if these forms do exist in the essence of the Absolute matter, all bodies would be identical in regard to the forms of darkness. This, however, is contradicted by daily experience. The cause of the forms of darkness, therefore, is not the Absolute matter. And as the difference of forms cannot be assigned to any other cause, it follows that they are due to the various illuminations of the Abstract Light. Forms of light and darkness both owe their existence to the Abstract Light. The third element of a material body—the obscure atom or essence—is nothing but a necessary aspect of the affirmation of light. The body as a whole, therefore, is completely dependent on the Primal Light. The whole Universe is really a continuous series of circles of existence, all depending on the original Light. Those nearer to the source receive more illumination than those more distant. All varieties of existence in each circle, and the circles themselves, are illuminated through an infinite number of medium-illuminations, which preserve some forms of existence by the help of " conscious light " (as in the case of man, animal and plant), and some without it (as in the case of minerals and primary elements). The immense panorama of diversity which we call the Universe, is, therefore, a vast shadow of the infinite variety in intensity of direct or indirect illuminations and rays of the Primary Light. Things are, so to speak, fed by their respective illuminations to which they constantly move, with a lover's passion, in order to drink more and more of the original fountain of Light. The world is an eternal drama of love. The different planes of being are as follow :—

The Plane of Primal Light.
1. The Plane of Intellects— the parent of the heavens.
2. The Plane of the Soul.
3. The Plane of Form.

1. The Plane of ideal form——
2. The Plane of material forms:—

1. The Plane of the haevens.
2. The Plane of the elements:—

(a) The heavens.
(b) The elements:–
  1. Simple elements.
  2. Compounds:—
    I. Mineral kingdom
    II. Vegetable kingdom.
    III. Animal kingdom.

(a) Simple elements.
(b) Compounds:—
  I. Mineral kingdom
  II. Vegetable kingdom.
  III. Animal kingdom.

Having briefly indicated the general nature of Being, we now proceed to a more detailed examination of the world-process. All that is not-light is divided into:—

(1) Eternal, e. g., Intellects, Souls of heavenly bodies, heavens, simple elements, time, motion.

(2) Contingent, e.g., Compounds of various elements. The motion of the heavens is eternal, and makes up the various cycles of the Universe. It is due to the intense longing of the heaven-soul to receive illumination from the source of all light. The matter of which the heavens are constructed is completely free from the operation of chemical processes, incidental to the grosser forms of the not-light. Every heaven has its own matter peculiar to it alone. Likewise the heavens differ from one another in the direction of their motion; and the difference is explained by the fact that the beloved, or the sustaining

illumination, is different in each case. Motion is only an aspect of time. It is the summing up of the elements of time, which, as externalised, is motion. The distinction of past, present, and future is made only for the sake of convenience, and does not exist in the nature of time.[1] We cannot conceive the beginning of time; for the supposed beginning would be a point of time itself. Time and motion, therefore, are both eternal.

There are three primordial elements—water, earth, and wind. Fire, according to the Ishrāqīs, is only burning wind. The combinations of these elements, under various heavenly influences, assume various forms—fluidity, gaseousness, solidity. This transformation of the original elements constitutes the process of " making and unmaking " which pervades the entire sphere of the not-light, raising the different forms of existence higher and higher, and bringing them nearer and nearer to the illuminating forces. All the phenomena of nature—rain, clouds, thunder, meteors—are the various workings of this immanent principle of motion, and are explained by the direct or indirect operation of the Primal Light on things, which differ from one another in their capacity of receiving more or less illumination. The Universe, in one word, is a petrified desire; a crystallised longing after light.

But is it eternal ? The Universe is a manifestation of the illuminative power which constitutes the

[1] Sh. An. fol. 34.

essential nature of the Primal Light. In so far, therefore, as it is a manifestation, it is only a dependent being, and consequently not eternal. But in another sense it is eternal. All the different spheres of being exist by the illuminations and rays of the Eternal light. There are some illuminations which are directly eternal; while there are other fainter ones, the appearance of which depends on the combination of other illuminations and rays. The existence of these is not eternal in the same sense as the existence of the pre-existing parent illuminations. The existence of colour, for instance, is contingent in comparison to that of the ray, which manifests colour when a dark body is brought before an illuminating body. The Universe, therefore, though contingent as manifestation, is eternal by the eternal character of its source. Those who hold the non-eternity of the Universe argue on the assumption of the possibility of a complete induction. Their argument proceeds in the following manner :—

(1) Everyone of the Abyssinians is black;

therefore all Abyssinians are black.

(2) Every motion began at a definite moment;

therefore all motion must begin so.

But this mode of argumentation is vicious. It is quite impossible to state the major. One cannot collect all the Abyssinians past, present, and future, at one particular moment of time. Such a Universal, therefore, is impossible. Hence from the examination of individual Abyssinians, or particular instances of motion which fall within the pale of our experience, it is rash to infer that all Abyssinians are black, or all motion had a beginning in time.

Psychology

Motion and light are not concomitant in the case of bodies of a lower order. A piece of stone, for instance, though illuminated and hence visible, is not endowed with self-initiated movement. As we rise, however, in the scale of being, we find higher bodies, or organisms in which motion and light are associated together. The abstract illumination finds its best dwelling place in man. But the question arises whether the individual abstract illumination which we call the human soul, did or did not exist before its physical accompaniment. The founder of Ishrāqī Philosophy follows Avicenna in connection with this question, and uses the same arguments to show that the individual abstract illuminations cannot be held to have pre-existed, as so many units of light. The material categories of one and many cannot be applied to the abstract illumination which, in its essential nature, is neither one nor many; though it appears as many owing to the various degrees of illuminational receptivity in its material accompaniments. The relation between the abstract illumination, or soul and body, is not that of cause and effect; the bond of union between them is love. The body which longs for illumination, receives it through the soul; since its nature does not permit a direct communication between the source of light and itself. But the soul cannot transmit the directly received light to the dark solid body which, considering its attributes, stands on the opposite pole of being. In order to be related to each other, they require a medium between them, something standing midway between light and darkness. This medium is the animal soul—a hot, fine, transparent vapour which has its principal seat in the left cavity of the heart, but also circulates in all parts of the body. It is because of the partial identity of the animal soul with light that, in dark nights, land-animals run towards the burning fire; while sea-animals leave their aquatic abodes in order to enjoy the beautiful sight of the moon. The ideal of man, therefore, is to rise higher and higher in the scale of being, and to receive more and more illumination which gradually brings complete freedom from the world of forms. But how is this ideal to be realised ? By knowledge and action. It is the transformation of both understanding and will, the union of action and contemplation, that actualises the highest ideal of man. Change your attitude towards the Universe, and adopt the line of conduct necessitated by the change. Let us briefly consider these means of realisation :—

(*a*) *Knowledge.* When the Abstract illumination associates itself with a higher organism, it works out its development by the operation of certain faculties —the powers of light, and the powers of darkness.

The former are the five external senses, and the five internal senses—sensorium, conception, imagination, understanding, and memory; the latter are the powers of growth, digestion, etc. But such a division of faculties is only convenient. "One faculty can be the source of all operations."[1] There is only one power in the middle of the brain, though it receives different names from different standpoints. The mind is a unity which, for the sake of convenience, is regarded as multiplicity. The power residing in the middle of the brain must be distinguished from the abstract illumination which constitutes the real essence of man. The philosopher of illumination appears to draw a distinction between the active mind and the essentially inactive soul; yet he teaches that, in some mysterious way, all the various faculties are connected with the soul.

The most original point in his psychology of intellection, however, is his theory of vision.[2] The ray of light which is supposed to come out of the eye must be either substance or quality. If quality, it cannot be transmitted from one substance (eye) to another substance (visible body). If, on the other hand, it is a substance, it moves either consciously, or impelled by its inherent nature. Conscious movement would make it an animal perceiving other things. The perceiver in this case would be the ray, not man. If the movement of the ray is an attribute of its nature, there is no reason why its movement

[1] Sh. An. fol. 57 b.
[2] Sh. An. fol. 60 b.

should be peculiar to one direction, and not to all. The ray of light, therefore, cannot be regarded as coming out of the eye. The followers of Aristotle hold that in the process of vision images of objects are printed on the eye. This view is also erroneous; since images of big things cannot be printed on a small space. The truth is that when a thing comes before the eye, an illumination takes place, and the mind sees the object through that illumination. When there is no veil between the object and the normal sight, and the mind is ready to perceive, the act of vision must take place; since this is the law of things. "All vision is illumination; and we see things in God". Berkley explained the relativity of our sight-perceptions with a view to show that the ultimate ground of all ideas is God. The Ishrāqī Philosopher has the same object in view, though his theory of vision is not so much an explanation of the sight-process as a new way of looking at the fact of vision.

Besides sense and reason, however, there is another source of knowledge called "Dhauq"—the inner perception which reveals non-temporal and non-spatial planes of being. The study of philosophy or the habit of reflecting on pure concepts, combined with the practice of virtue, leads to the upbringing of this mysterious sense, which corroborates and corrects the conclusions of intellect.

(b) *Action.* Man as an active being has the following motive powers :

(a) Reason or the Angelic soul—the source of intelligence, discrimination, and love of knowledge.

(b) The beast-soul which is the source of anger, courage, dominance, and ambition.

(c) The animal soul which is the source of lust, hunger and sexual passion.

The first leads to wisdom; the second and third, if controlled by reason, lead respectively to bravery and chastity. The harmonious use of all results in the virtue of justice. The possibility of spiritual progress by virtue, shows that this world is the best possible world. Things as existent are neither good nor bad. It is misuse or limited standpoint that makes them so. Still the fact of evil cannot be denied. Evil does exist; but it is far less in amount than good. It is peculier only to a part of the world of darkness; while there are other parts of the Universe which are quite free from the taint of evil. The sceptic who attributes the existence of evil to the creative agency of God, presupposes resemblance between human and divine action, and does not see that nothing existent is free in his sense of the word. Divine activity cannot be regarded as the creator of evil in the same sense as we regard some forms of human activity as the cause of evil.[1]

It is, then, by the union of knowledge and virtue that the soul frees itself from the world of darkness. As we know more and more of the nature of things, we are brought closer and closer to the

---

[1] Sh.An fol. 92b.

world of light ; and the love of that world becomes more and more intense. The stages of spiritual development are infinite, since the degrees of love are infinite. The principal stages, however, are as follows :—

(1) The stage of *"I"*. In this stage feeling of personality is most predominant, and the spring of human action is generally selfishness.

(2) The stage of *"Thou art not"*. Complete absorption in one's own deep self to the entire forgetfulness of everything external.

(3) The stage of *"I am not"*. This stage is the necessary result of the second.

(4) The stage of *"Thou art"*. The absolute negation of *"I"*, and the affirmation of *"Thou"*, which means complete resignation to the will of God.

(5) The stage of *"I am not ; and Thou art not"*. The complete negation of both the terms of thought — the state of cosmic consciousness.

Each stage is marked by more or less intense illuminations, which are accompanied by some indescribable sounds. Death does not put an end to the spiritual progress of the soul. The individual souls, after death, are not unified into one soul, but continue different from each other in proportion to the illumination they received during their companionship with physical organisms. The Philosopher of illumination anticipates Leibniz's doctrine of the Identity of Indiscernibles, and holds that no two souls can be completely similar to each other.[1]

[1] Sh. An. fol. 82.

When the material machinery which it adopts for the purpose of acquiring gradual illumination, is exhausted, the soul probably takes up another body determined by the experiences of the previous life; and rises higher and higher in the different spheres of being, adopting forms peculiar to those spheres, until it reaches its destination—the state of absolute negation. Some souls probably come back to this world in order to make up their deficiencies.[1] The doctrine of transmigration cannot be proved or disproved from a purely logical standpoint; though it is a probable hypothesis to account for the future destiny of the soul. All souls are thus constantly journeying towards their common source, which calls back the whole Universe when this journey is over, and starts another cycle of being to reproduce, in almost all respects, the history of the preceding cycles.

Such is the philosophy of the great Persian martyr. He is, properly speaking, the first Persian systematiser who recognises the elements of truth in all the aspects of Persian speculation, and skilfully synthesises them in his own system. He is a pantheist in so far as he defines God as the sum total of all sensible and ideal existence.[2] To him, unlike some of his Ṣūfī predecessors, the world is something real, and the human soul a distinct individuality. With the orthodox theologian, he maintains that the ultimate cause of every phenomenon, is the Absolute

[1] Sh. An. fol. 87 b.
[2] Sh. An. fol. 81 b.

Light whose illumination forms the very essence of the Universe. In his psychology he follows Avicenna, but his treatment of this branch of study is more systematic and more empirical. As an ethical philosopher, he is a follower of Aristotle whose doctrine of the mean he explains and illustrates with great thoroughness. Above all he modifies and transforms the traditional Neo-Platonism, into a thoroughly Persian system of thought which, not only approaches Plato, but also spiritualises the old Persian Dualism. No Persian thinker is more alive to the necessity of explaining all the aspects of objective existence in reference to his fundamental principles. He constantly appeals to experience, and endeavours to explain even the physical phenomena in the light of his theory of illumination. In his system objectivity, which was completely swallowed up by the exceedingly subjective character of extreme pantheism, claims its due again, and, having been subjected to a detailed examination, finds a comprehensive explanation. No wonder then that this acute thinker succeeded in founding a system of thought, which has always exercised the greatest fascination over minds—uniting speculation and emotion in perfect harmony. The narrow-mindedness of his contemporaries gave him the title of "Maqtūl" (the killed one), signifying that he was not to be regarded as "Shahīd" (Martyr); but succeeding generations of Ṣūfīs and philosophers have always given him the profoundest veneration.

I may here notice a less spiritual form of the

Ishrāqī mode of thought. Nasafī[1] describes a phase of Ṣūfī thought which reverted to the old materialistic dualism of Mānī. The advocates of this view hold that light and darkness are essential to each other. They are, in reality, two rivers which mix with each other like oil and milk [2] out of which arises the diversity of things. The ideal of human action is freedom from the taint of darkness; and the freedom of light from darkness means the self-consciousness of light as light.

2. REALITY AS THOUGHT—AL-JILI

Al-Jīlī was born in 767 A.H., as he himself says in one of his verses, and died in 811 A.H. He was not a prolific writer like Shaikh Muhy al-Dīn ibn 'Arabī whose mode of thought seems to have greatly influenced his teaching. He combined in himself poetical imagination and philosophical genius, but his poetry is no more than a vehicle for his mystical and metaphsical doctrines. Among other books he wrote a commentry on Shaikh Muhy al-Dīn ibn 'Arabī's al-Futūḥāt al-Makkiya, a commentary on Bismillāh, and the famous work Insān al-Kāmil (printed in Cairo).

Essence pure and simple, he says, is the thing to which names and attributes are given, whether it is existent actually or ideally. The existent is of two species:—

---

[1] Maqsadi Aqsā; fol. 21 a.
[2] Maqsadi Aqsā; fol. 21 a.

(1) The Existent in Absoluteness or Pure existence—Pure Being—God.

(2) The existence joined with non-existence—Creation—Nature.

The Essence of God or Pure Thought cannot be understood; no words can express it, for it is beyond all relation and knowledge is relation. The intellect flying through the fathomless empty space pierces through the veil of names and attributes, traverses the vasty sphere of time, enters the domain of the non-existent and finds the Essence of Pure Thought to be an existence which is non-existence—a sum of contradictions.[1] It has two (accidents); eternal life in all past time and eternal life in all future time. It has two (qualities), God and creation. It has two (definitions), uncreatableness and creatableness. It has two names, God and man. It has two faces, the manifested (this world) and the unmanifested (the next world). It has two effects, necessity and possibility. It has two points of view; from the first it is non-existent for itself but existent for what is not itself; from the second it is existent for itself and non-existent for what is not itself.

Name, he says, fixes the named in the understanding, pictures it in the mind, presents it in the imagination and keeps it in the memory. It is the outside or the husk, as it were, of the named; while the named is the inside or the pith. Some names do not exist in reality but exist in name only as "Anqā"

---

[1] Insān al-Kāmil, Vol. 1, p. 10.

(a fabulous bird). It is a name the object of which does not exist in reality. Just as "'Anqā" is absolutely non-existent, so God is absolutely present, although He cannot be touched and seen. The " 'Anqā" exists only in idea while the object of the name "Allāh" exists in reality and can be known like " 'Anqā" only through its names and attributes. The name is a mirror which reveals all the secrets of the Absolute Being; it is a light through the agency of which God sees Himself. Al-Jīlī here approaches the Isma'īlia view that we should seek the Named through the Name.

In order to understand this passage we should bear in mind the three stages of the development of Pure Being, enumerated by him. He holds that the Absolute existence or Pure Being, when it leaves its absoluteness undergoes three stages;—(1) Oneness. (2) He-ness. (3) I-ness. In the first stage there is an absence of all attributes and relations, yet it is called one, and, therefore, oneness marks one step away from the absoluteness. In the second stage Pure Being is set free from all manifestation, while the third stage, I-ness, is nothing but an external manifestation of the He-ness, or, as Hegel would say, it is the self-diremption of God. This third stage is the sphere of the name Allāh; here the darkness of Pure Being is illuminated, nature comes to the front, the Absolute Being has become conscious. He says further that the name Allāh is the stuff of all the perfections of the different phases of Divinity, and in the second stage of the progress of Pure

Being, all that is the result of Divine self-diremption was potentially contained within the titanic grasp of this name which, in the third stage of the development, objectified itself, became a mirror in which God reflected Himself, and thus by its crystallisation dispelled all the gloom of the Absolute Being.

In correspondence with these three stages of the absolute development, the perfect man has three stages of spiritual training. But in his case the process of development must be the reverse; because his is the process of ascent, while the Absolute Being had undergone essentially a process of descent. In the first stage of his spiritual progress he meditates on the name, studies nature on which it is sealed; in the second stage he steps into the sphere of the Attribute, and in the third stage enters the sphere of the Essence. It is here that he becomes the Perfect Man; his eye becomes the eye of God, his word the word of God and his life the life of God—participates in the general life of Nature and "sees into the life of things".

To turn now to the nature of the attribute. His views on this most interesting question are very important, because it is here that his doctrine fundamentally differs from Hindu Idealism. He defines attribute as an agency which gives us a knowledge of the state of things.[1] Elsewhere he says that this distinction of attribute from the

[1] Insān al-Kāmil; Vol. I, p. 22.

underlying reality is tenable only in the sphere of the manifested, because here every attribute is regarded as the other of the reality in which it is supposed to inhere. This otherness is due to the existence of combination and disintegration in the sphere of the manifested. But the distinction is untenable in the domain of the unmanifested, because there is no combination or disintegration there. It should be observed how widely he differs from the advocates of the Doctrine of "Māyā". He believes that the material world has real existence; it is the outward husk of the real being, no doubt, but this outward husk is not the less real. The cause of the phenomenal world, according to him, is not a real entity hidden behind the sum of attributes, but it is a conception furnished by the mind so that there may be no difficulty in understanding the material world. Berkely and Fichte will so far agree with our author, but his view leads him to the most characteristically Hegelian doctrine —identity of thought and being. In the thirty-seventh chapter of the second volume of Insān al-Kāmil, he clearly says that idea is the stuff of which this universe is made ; thought, idea, notion is the material of the structure of nature. While laying stress on this doctrine he says, "Dost thou not look to thine own belief ? Where is the reality in which the so-called Divine attributes inhere ? It is but the idea."[1] Hence nature is nothing but a crystallised idea. He gives his hearty assent to the results

[1] Insān al-Kāmil, Vol. II, p. 26.

of Kant's *Critique of Pure Reason* ; but, unlike him, he makes this very idea the essence of the Universe. Kant's *Ding an sich* to him is a pure nonentity ; there is nothing behind the collection of attributes. The attributes are the real things, the material world is but the objectification of the Absolute Being ; it is the other self of the Absolute— another which owes its existence to the principle of difference in the nature of the Absolute itself. Nature is the idea of God, a something necessary for His knowledge of Himself. While Hegel calls his doctrine the identity of thought and being. Al-Jīlī calls it the indentity of attribute and reality. It should be noted that the author's phrase, "world of attributes", which he uses for the material world is slightly misleading. What he really holds is that the distinction of attribute and reality is merely phenomenal, and does not at all exist in the nature of things. It is useful, because it facilitates our understanding of the world around us, but it is not at all real. It will be understood that Al-Jīlī recognises the truth of Empirical Idealism only tentatively, and does not admit the absoluteness of the distinction. These remarks should not lead us to understand that Al-Jīlī does not believe in the objective reality of the thing in itself. He does believe in it, but then he advocates its unity, and says that the meterial world is the thing in itself ; it is the "other", the external expression of the thing in itself The *Ding an sich* and its external expression or the production of its self-diremption, are really indentical, though we discriminate between them in order to facilitate our understanding of the universe. If they are not identical, he says, how could one manifest the other? In one word, he means by *Ding an sich,* the Pure, the Absolute Being, and seeks it through its manifestation or external expression. He says that as long as we do not realise the identity of attribute and reality, the material world or the world of attributes seems to be a veil; but when the doctrine is brought home to us the veil is removed; we see the Essence itself everywhere, and find that all the attributes are but ourselves. Nature then appears in her true light; all otherness is removed and we are one with her. The aching prick of curiosity ceases, and the inquisitive attitude of our minds in replaced by a state of philosophic calm. To the person who has realised this identity, discoveries of science bring no new information, and religion with her role of supernatural authority has nothing to say. This is the spiritual emancipation.

Let us now see how he classifies the different divine names and attributes which have received expression in nature or crystallised Divinity. His classification is as follows :—

(1) The names and attributes of God as He is in Himself (Allāh, The One, The Odd, The Light, The Truth, The Pure, The Living).

(2) The names and attributes of God as the source of all glory (The Great and High, The All-powerful).

(3) The names and attributes of God as all Perfection (The Creator, The Benefactor, The First, The Last).

(4) The names and attributes of God as all Beauty (The Uncreatable, The Painter, The Merciful, The Origin of all). Each of these names and attributes has its own particular effect by which it illuminates the soul of the perfect man and Nature. How these illuminations take place, and how they reach the soul is not explained by Al-Jīlī. His silence about these matters throws into more relief the mystical portion of his views and implies the necessity of spiritual Directorship.

Before considering Al-Jīlī's views of particular Divine Names and Attributes, we should note that his conception of God, implied in the above classification, is very similar to that of Schleiermacher. While the German theologian reduces all the divine artributes to one single attribute of Power, our author sees the danger of advancing a God free from all attributes, yet recognises with Schleiermacher that in Himself God is an unchangeable unity, and that His attributes " are nothing more than views of Him from different human standpoints, the various appearances which the one changeless cause presents to our finite intelligence according as we look at it from different sides of the spiritual landscape."[1] In His absolute existence He is beyond the limitation of names and attributes, but when He externalises Himself, when He leaves His absoluteness, when nature is born, names and attributes appear sealed on her very fabric.

[1] Matheson's *Aids to the Study of German Theology*, p. 43.

We now proceed to consider what he teaches about particular Divine Names and Attributes. The first Essential Name is Allāh (Divinity) which means the sum of all the realities of existence with their respective order in that sum. This name is applied to God as the only necessary existence. Divinity being the highest manifestation of Pure Being, the difference between them is that the latter is visible to the eye, but its *where* is invisible; while the traces of the former are visible, itself is invisible. By the very fact of her being crystallised divinity, Nature is not the real divinity; hence Divinity is invisible, and its traces in the form of Nature are visible to the eye. Divinity, as the author illustrates, is water; nature is crystallised water or ice; but ice is not water. The Essence is visible to the eye, (another proof of our author's Natural Realism or Absolute Idealism) although all its attributes are not known to us. Even its attributes are not known as they are in themselves, their shadows or effects only are known. For instance, charity itself is unknown, only its effect or the fact of giving to the poor, is known and seen. This is due to the attributes being incorporated in the very nature of the Essence. If the expression of the attributes in its real nature had been possible, its separation from the Essence would have been possible also. But there are some other Essential Names of God—The Absolute Oneness and Simple Oneness. The Absolute Oneness marks the first step of Pure Thought from the darkness of Cecity (the internal or the original Māyā of the

Vedānta) to the light of manifestation. Although this movement is not attended with any external manifestations, yet it sums up all of them under its hollow universality. Look at a wall, says the author, you see the whole wall; but you cannot see the individual pieces of the material that contribute to its formation. The wall is a unity—but a unity which comprehends diversity, so Pure Being is a unity but a unity which is the soul of diversity.

The third movement of the Absolute Being is Simple Oneness—a step attended with external manifestation. The Absolute Oneness is free from all particular names and attributes. The Oneness Simple takes on names and attributes, but there is no distinction between these attributes, one is the essence of the other. Divinity is similar to Simple Oneness, but its names and attributes are distinguished from one another and even contradictory, as generous is contradictory to revengeful.[1] The third step, or as Hegel would say, Voyage of the Being, has another appellation (Mercy). The First Mercy, the author says, is the evolution of the Universe from Himself and the manifestation of His own self

---

[1] This would seem very much like the idea of the phenomenal Brahma of the Vedānta. The Personal Creator or the Prajāpati of the Vedānta makes the third step of the Absolute Being or the Noumenal Brahma. Al-Jīlī seems to admit two kinds of Brahma—with or without qualities like the Samkara and Bādarayana. To him the process of creation is essentially a lowering of the Absolute Thought, which is Asat, in so far as it is absolute, and Sat, in so far as it is manifested and hence limited. Nowithstanding this Absolute Monism, he inclines to a view similar to that of Rāmānuja. He seems to admit the reality of the individual soul and seems to imply, unlike Samkara, that Iśwara and His worship are necessary even after the attainment of the Higher Knowledge.

in every atom of the result of His own self-diremption. Al-Jīlī makes this point clearer by an instance. He says that nature is frozen water and God is water. The real name of nature is God (Allāh); ice or condensed water is merely a borrowed appellation. Elsewhere he calls water the origin of knowledge, intellect, understanding, thought and idea. This instance leads him to guard against the error of looking upon God as immanent in nature, or running through the sphere of material existence. He says that immanence implies disparity of being; God is not immanent because He is Himself the existence. Eternal existence is the other self of God, it is the light through which He sees Himself. As the originator of an idea is existent in that idea, so God is present in nature. The difference between God and man, as one may say, is that His ideas materialise themselves, ours do not. It will be remembered here that Hegel would use the same line of argument in freeing himself from the accusation of Pantheism.

The attribute of Mercy is closely connected with the attribute of Providence. He defines it as the sum of all that existence stands in need of. Plants are supplied with water through the force of this name. The natural philosopher would express the same thing differently; he would speak of the same phenomena as resulting from the activity of a certain force of nature; Al-Jīlī would call it a manifestation of Providence; but, unlike the natural philosopher, he would not advocate the unknowability of that force. He would say that there is nothing behind it, it is the Absolute Being itself.

We have now finished all the essential names and attributes of God, and proceed to examine the nature of what existed before all things. The Arabian Prophet, says Al-Jili, was once questioned about the place of God before creation. He said that God, before the creation, existed in "Ama" (Blindness). It is the nature of this Blindness or primal darkness which we now proceed to examine. The investigation is particularly interesting, because the word translated into modern phraseology would be *"The Unconsciousness"*. This single word impresses upon us the foresightedness with which he anticipates metaphysical doctrines of modern Germany. He says that the Unconsciousness is the reality of all realities; it is the Pure Being without any descending movement; it is free from the attributes of God and creation; it does not stand in need of any name or quality, because it is beyond the sphere of relation. It is distinguished from the Absolute Oneness because the latter name is applied to the Pure Being in its process of coming down towards manifestation. It should, however, be remembered that when we speak of the priority of God and posteriority of creation, our words must not be understood as implying time; for there can be no duration of time or separateness between God and His creation. Time, continuity in space and time, are themselves creations, and how can a piece of creation intervene between God and

His creation. Hence our words before, after, where, whence, etc., in this sphere of thought, should not be construed to imply time or space. The real thing is beyond the grasp of human conceptions; no category of material existence can be applicable to it; because, as Kant would say, the laws of phenomena cannot be spoken of as obtaining in the sphere of noumena.

We have already noticed that man in his progress towards perfection has three stages: the first is the meditation of the name which the author calls the illumination of names. He remarks that "When God illuminates a certain man by the light of His names, the man is destroyed under the dazzling splendour of that name: and "when thou calleth God, the call is responded to by the man". The effect of this illumination would be, in Schopenhauer's language, the destruction of the individual will, yet it must not be confounded with physical death; because the individual goes on living and moving like the spinning wheel, as Kapila would say, after he has become one with Prakriti. It is here that the individual cries out in pantheistic mood:—She was I and I was she and there was none to separate us."[1]

The second stage of the spiritual training is what he calls the illumination of the Attribute. This illumination makes the perfect man receive the attributes of God in their real nature in proportion to the power of receptivity possessed by him—a fact

[1] Insān al-Kāmil, Vol. I, p. 40.

which classifies men according to the magnitude of this light resulting from the illumination. Some men receive illumination from the divine attribute of Life, and thus participate in the soul of the Universe. The effect of this light is soaring in the air, walking on water, changing the magnitude of things. (as Christ so often did). In this wise the perfect man receives illumination from all the Divine attributes, crosses the sphere of the name and the attribute, and steps into the domain of the Essence—Absolute Existence.

As we have already seen, the Absolute Being, when it leaves its absoluteness, has three voyages to undergo, each voyage being a process of particularisation of the bare universality of the Absolute Essence. Each of these three movements appears under a new Essential Name which has its own peculiar illuminating effect upon the human soul. Here is the end of our author's spiritual ethics; *man has become perfect,* he has amalgamated himself with the Absolute Being, or *has learnt what Hegel calls The Absolute Philosophy.* "He becomes the paragon of perfection, the object of worship, the preserver of the Universe".[1] He is the point where Man-ness and God-ness become one, and result in the birth of the god-man.

How the perfect man reaches this height of spiritual development, the author does not tell us; but he says that at every stage he has a peculiar experience in which there is not even a trace of doubt or agitation. The instrument of this experience

[1] Insān al Kāmil, Vol, I, p. 48.

is what he calls the *Qalb* (heart), a word very difficult of definition. He gives a very mystical diagram of the *Qalb*, and explains it by saying that it is the eye which sees the names, the attributes and the Absolute Being successively It owes its existence to a mysterious combination of soul and mind ; and becomes by its very nature the organ for the recognition of the ultimate realities of existence. All that the "heart", or the source of what the Vedānta calls the Higher Knowledge, reveals, is not seen by the individual as something separate from and heterogeneous to himself ; what is shown to him through this agency is his own reality, his own deep being. This characteristic of the agency differentiates it from the intellect, the object of which is always different and separate from the individual exercising that faculty. But the spiritual experience, according to the Ṣūfīs of this school, is not permanent ; moments of spiritual vision, says Matthew Arnold,[1] cannot be at our command. The god-man is he who has known the mystery of his own being, who has realised himself as god-man ; but when that particular spiritual realisation is over, man is man and God is God. Had the experience been permanent, a great moral force would have been lost and society overturned.

Let us now sum up Al-Jīlī's *Doctrine of the Trinity*. We have seen the three movements of the Absolute Being, or the first three categories of Pure

[1] "We cannot kindle, when we will,
　The fire which in the heart resides."

Being ; we have also seen that the third movement is attended with external manifestation, which is the self-diremption of the Essence into God and man. This separation makes a gap which is filled by the perfect man, who shares in both the Divine and the human attributes. He holds that the perfect man is the preserver of the Universe ; hence in his view, the appearance of the perfect man is a necessary condition for the continuation of nature. It is easy, therefore, to understand that in the god-man, the Absolute Being which has left its absoluteness, returns into itself; and, but for the god-man, it could not have done so ; for then there would have been no nature, and consequently no light through which God could have seen Himself. The light through the agency of which God sees Himself is due to the principle of difference in the nature of the Absolute Being itself. He recognises this principle in the following verses :—

> If you say that God is one, you are right ; but if you say that He is two, this is also true.
>
> If you say no, but He is three, you are right, for this is the real nature of man.[1]

The *perfect man*, then, is the joining link. On the one hand he receives illumination from all the Essential names, on the other hand all Divine attributes reappear in him. These attributes are :—

1. Independent life or existence.

---

[1] Insān al Kāmil, vol. I, p. 8.

2. Knowledge which is a form of life, as he proves from a verse from the Qur'ān.

3. Will—the principle of particularisation, or the manifestation of Being. He defines it as the illumination of the knowledge of God according to the requirements of the Essence; hence it is a particular form of knowledge. It has nine manifestations, all of which are different names for love; the last is the love in which the lover and the beloved, the knower and the known merge into each other, and become identical. This form of love, he says, is the Absolute Essence; as Christianity teaches, God is love. He guards here, against the error of looking upon the individual act of will as uncaused. Only the act of the universal will is uncaused; hence he implies the Hegelian Doctrine of Freedom, and holds that the acts of man are both free and determined.

4. Power, which expresses itself in self-diremption, i.e., creation. He controverts Shaikh Muḥy al-Dīn ibn 'Arabī's position that the Universe existed before the creation in the knowledge of God. He says, this would imply that God did not create it out of nothing, and holds that the Universe, before its existence as an idea, existed in the self of God.

5. The word or the reflected being. Every possibility is the word of God; hence nature is the materialisation of the word of God. It has different names—the tangible word, the sum of the realities of man, the arrangement of the Divinity, the spread

of Oneness, the expression of the Unknown, the phases of Beauty, the trace of names and attributes, and the object of God's knowledge.

6. The Power of hearing the inaudible.

7. The Power of seeing the invisible.

8. Beauty—that which seems least beautiful in nature (the reflected beauty) is in its real existence, beauty. Evil is only relative, it has no real existence; sin is merely a relative deformity.

9. Glory or beauty in its intensity.

10. Perfection, which is the unknowable essence of God and therefore Unlimited and Infinite.

CHAPTER VI

LATER PERSIAN THOUGHT

Under the rude Tartar invaders of Persia, who could have no sympathy with independent thought, there could be no progress of ideas. Ṣūfīism, owing to its association with religion, went on systematising old and evolving new ideas. But philosophy proper was distasteful to the Tartar. Even the development of Islamic law suffered a check ; since the Ḥanafite law was the acme of human reason to the Tartar, and further subtleties of legal interpretation were disagreeable to his brain. Old schools of thought lost their solidarity, and many thinkers left their native country to find more favourable conditions elsewhere. In the 16th Century we find Persian Aristotelians—Dastūr Isfahānī, Hīr Bud, Munīr and Kāmrān—travelling in India, where the Emperor Akbar was drawing upon Zoroastrianism to form a new faith for himself and his courtiers, who were mostly Persians. No great thinker, however, appeared in Persia until the 17th Century, when the acute Mulla Ṣadra of Shīrāz upheld his philosophical system with all the vigour of his powerful logic. With Mulla Ṣadra, Reality is all things, yet is none of them, and true knowledge consists in the identity of the subject and the object. De Gobineau thinks that the philosophy of Ṣadra is a mere revival of Avicennaism. He, however, ignores the fact that Mulla Ṣadra's doctrine of the identity of subject and object constitutes the final step which the Persian intellect took towards complete monism. It is, moreover, the Philosophy of Ṣadra which is the source of the metaphysics of early Bābism.

But the movement towards Platonism is best illustrated in Mulla Hādī of Sabzwār, who flourished in the 18th Century, and is believed by his countrymen to be the greatest of modern Persian thinkers. As a specimen of comparatively recent Persian speculation, I may briefly notice here the views of this great thinker, as set forth in his Asrār al-Ḥikam (published in Persia). A glance at his philosophical teaching reveals three fundamental conceptions which are indissolubly associated with the Post-Islamic Persian thought :—

1. The idea of the Absolute Unity of the Real which is described as "Light".

2. The idea of evolution which is dimly visible in Zoroaster's doctrine of the destiny of the human soul, and receives further expansion and systematisation by Persian Neo-Platonists and Ṣūfī thinkers.

3. The idea of a medium between the Absolute Real and the not-Real.

It is highly interesting to note how the Persian mind gradually got rid of the Emanation theory of Neo-Platonism, and reached a purer notion of Plato's

Philosophy. The Arab Muhammadans of Spain, by a similar process of elimination, reached through the same medium (Neo-Platonism) a truer conception of the Philosophy of Aristotle—a fact which illustrates the genius of the two races. Lewes, in his Biographical History of Philosophy, remarks that the Arabs eagerly took up the study of Aristotle, simply because Plato was not presented to them. I am, however, inclined to think that the Arab genius was thoroughly practical; hence Plato's philosophy would have been distasteful to them even if it had been presented in its true light. Of the systems of Greek philosophy, Neo-Platonism, I believe, was the only one which was presented in its completeness to the Muslim world; yet patient critical research led the Arab from Plotinus to Aristotle, and the Persian to Plato. This is singularly illustrated in the Philosophy of Mulla Hādī, who recognises no Emanations, and approaches the Platonic conception of the Real. He illustrates, moreover, how philosophical speculation in Persia, as in all countries where Physical Science either does not exist or is not studied, is finally absorbed by religion. The "Essence", i.e., the metaphysical cause as distinguished from the scientific cause, which means the sum of antecedent conditions, must gradually be transformed into "Personal Will" (cause, in a religious sense) in the absence of any other notion of cause. And this is, perhaps, the deeper reason why Persian philosophies have always ended in religion.

Let us now turn to Mulla Hādī's system of thought. He teaches that Reason has two aspects ; (*a*) Theoretical, the object of which is Philosophy and Mathematics ; (*b*) Practical, the object of which is Domestic Economy, Politics, etc. Philosophy proper comprises the knowledge of the beginning of things, the end of things, and the knowledge of the Self. It also includes the knowledge of the law of God—which is identical with religion. In order to understand the origin of things, we should subject to a searching analysis the various phenomena of the Universe. Such an analysis reveals that there are three original principles.[1]

(1) The Real—Light.
(2) The Shadow.
(3) The not-Real—Darkness.

The Real is absolute, and necessary as distinguished from the "Shadow", which is relative and contingent. In its nature it is absolutely good ; and the proposition, that it is good, is self-evident.[2] All forms of potential existence, before they are actualised by the Real, are open to both existence or non-existence, and the possibilities of their existence or non-existence are exactly equal. It, therefore, follows that the Real which actualises the potential is not itself non-existence ; since non-existence operating on non-existence cannot produce actuality.[3] Mulla Hādī, in his conception of the Real as the

[1] Asrār al-Hikam : p. 6.
[2] Ibid. p. 8.
[3] Ibid. p 8.

operator, modifies Plato's statical conception of the Universe, and, following Aristotle, looks upon his Real as the immovable source and the object of all motion. "All things in the Universe", he says, "love perfection, and are moving towards their final ends —minerals towards vegetables, vegetables towards animals, and animals towards man. And observe how man passes through all these stages in the mother's womb."[1] The mover as mover is either the source or the object of motion or both. In any case the mover must be either movable or immovable. The proposition, that all movers must be themselves movable, leads to infinite regress—which must stop at the immovable mover, the source and the final object of all motion. The Real, moreover, is a pure unity; for if there is a plurality of Reals, one would limit the other. The Real as creator also cannot be conceived as more than one; since a plurality of creators would mean a plurality of worlds which must be circular touching one another, and this again implies vacuum which is immpossible.[2] Regarded as an essence, therefore, the Real is one. But it is also many, from a different standpoint. It is life, power, love; though we cannot say that these qualities inhere in it—they are it, and it is them. Unity does not mean oneness, its essence consists in the "dropping of all relations". Unlike the Ṣūfīs and other thinkers, Mulla Hādī holds and tries to show

[1] Asrār al-Ḥikam : p. 10.
[2] Ibid. pp. 28-29.

that belief in multiplicity is not inconsistent with belief in unity ; since the visible " many " is nothing more than a manifestation of the names and attributes of the Real. These attributes are the various forms of "Knowledge" which constitutes the very essence of the Real. To speak, however, of the attributes of the Real is only a verbal convenience ; since "defining the Real is applying the category of number to it"—an absurd process which endeavours to bring the unrelated into the sphere of the related. The Universe, with all its variety, is the shadow of the various names and attributes of the Real or the Absolute Light. It is Reality unfolded, the "Be", or the word of Light.[1] Visible multiplicity is the illumination of Darkness, or the actualisation of Nothing. Things are different because we see them, as it were, through glasses of different colours—the Ideas. In this connection Hādī approvingly quotes the poet Jāmī who has given the most beautiful poetic expression to Plato's Doctrine of Ideas in verses which can be thus translated :—

"The ideas are glasses of various colours in which the Sun of Reality reflects itself, and makes itself visible through them according as they are red, yellow or blue."[2]

In his Psychology he mostly follows Avicenna. but his treatment of the subject is more thorough and systematic. He classifies the soul in the following manner :—

[1] Asrār al-Hikam : p. 151.
[2] Ibid. p. 6.

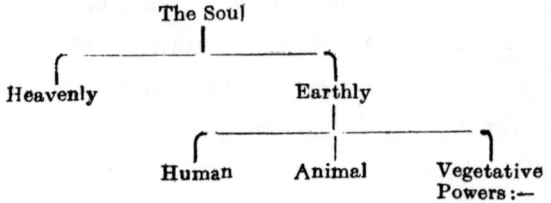

Vegetative Powers:—
1. Preserving the individual.
2. Prefecting the individual.
3. Perpetuating the species.

The animal soul has three powers:—

1. External senses } Perception.
2. Internal senses }
3. Power of motion which includes:
   (a) Voluntary motion.
   (b) Involuntary motion.

The external senses are taste, touch, smell hearing and sight. The sound exists outside the ear, and not inside as some thinkers have held. For if it does not exist outside the ear, it is not possible to perceive its direction and distance. Hearing and sight are superior to other senses, and sight is superior to hearing; since:—

(1) The eye can perceive distant things.

(2) Its perception is light, which is the best of all attributes.

(3) The construction of the eye is more complicated and delicate than that of the ear.

(4) The perceptions of sight are things which actually exist while those of hearing resemble non-existence.

The internal senses are as follow :

(1) The Common Sense—the tablet of the mind. It is like the Prime Minister of the mind sending out

five spies (external senses) to bring in news from the external world. When we say "this white thing is sweet", we perceive whiteness and sweetness by sight and taste, respectively, but that both the attributes exist in the same thing is decided by the Common Sense. The line made by a falling drop, so far as the eye is concerned, is nothing but the drop. But what is the line which we see ? To account for such a phenomenon, says Hādī, it is necessary to postulate another sense which perceives the lengthening of the falling drop into a line.

(2) The faculty which preserves the perceptions of the Common Sense—images and not ideas like the memory. The judgment that whiteness and sweetness exist in the same thing is completed by this faculty ; since, if it does not preserve the image of the subject Common Sense cannot preceive the predicate.

(3) The power which preceives individual ideas. The sheep thinks of the enmity of the wolf, and runs away from him. Some forms of life lack this power, e.g., the moth which hurls itself against the candle-flame.

(4) Memory—the preserver of ideas.

(5) The power of combining images and ideas, e.g. the winged man. When this faculty works under the guidance of the power which perceives individual ideas, it is called Imagination ; when it works under the control of Intellect, it is called Conception.

But it is the spirit which distinguishes man from other animals. This essence of humanity is a "unity", not oneness. It perceives the Universal by itself, and the particular through the external and the internal senses. It is the shadow of the Absolute Light, and like it manifests itself in various ways—comprehending multiplicity in its unity. There is no necessary relation between the spirit and the body. The former is non-temporal and non-spatial; hence it is changeless, and has the power of judging the visible multiplicity. In sleep the spirit uses the "ideal body" which functions like the physical body; in waking life it uses the ordinary physical body, It follows, therefore, that the spirit stands in need of neither, and uses both at will. Hādī does not follow Plato in his doctrine of transmigration, the different forms of which he refutes at length. The spirit to him is immortal, and reaches its original home—Absolute Light—by the gradual perfection of its faculties. The various stages of the development of reason are as follows:—

(a) Theoretical or Pure Reason—
　　1st Potential Reason.
　　2nd Perception of self-evident propositions.
　　3rd Actual Reason.
　　4th Perception of universal concepts.
(b) Practical Reason—
　　1st External Purification.
　　2nd Internal Purification.
　　3rd Formation of various habits.
　　4th Union with God.

Thus the spirit rises higher and higher in the scale of being, and finally shares in the eternity of the

Absolute Light by losing itself in its universality. "In itself non-existent, but existent in the eternal Friend: how wonderful that it *is* and *is not* at the same time." But is the spirit free to choose its course? Hādī criticises the Rationalists for their setting up man as an independent creator of evil, and accuses them of what he calls "veiled dualism". He holds that every object has two sides—"bright" side, and "dark" side. Things are combinations of light and darkness. All good flows from the side of light; evil proceeds from darkness. Man, therefore, is both free and determined.

But all the various lines of Persian thought once more find a synthesis in that great religious movement of Modern Persia—Bābism or Bahāism, which began as a Shī'ah sect, with Mirzā 'Alī Muḥammad Bāb of Shīrāz (b. 1820), and became less and less Islamic in character with the progress of orthodox persecutions. The origin of the philosophy of this wonderful sect must be sought in the Shī'ah sect of the Shaikhīs, the founder of which, Shaikh Aḥmad, was enthusiastic student of Mulla Ṣadrā's Philosophy, on which he had written several commentaries. This sect differed from the ordinary Shī'ahs in holding that belief in an ever present Medium between the absent Imām (the 12th Head of the Church, whose manifestation is anxiously expected by the Shī'ahs), and the Church is a fundamental principle of the Shī'ah religion. Shaikh Aḥmad claimed to be such a Medium; and when, after the death of the second

Shaikhī Medium—Ḥājī Kāzim—the Shaikhīs were anxiously expecting the manifestation of the new Medium, Mirza 'Alī Muḥammad Bāb, who had attended the lectures of Ḥājī Kāzim at Karbalā, proclaimed himself the expected Medium, and many Shaikhīs accepted him.

The young Persian seer looks upon Reality as an essence which brooks no distinction of substance and attribute. The first bounty or self-expansion of the Ultimate Essence, he says, is Existence. "Existence" is the "known", the "known" is the essence of "knowledge"; "knowledge" is "will"; and "will" is "love". Thus from Mulla Ṣadrā's identity of the known and the knower, he passes to his conception of the Real as Will and Love. This Primal Love, which he regards as the essence of the Real, is the cause of the manifestation of the Universe which is nothing more than the self-expansion of Love. The word creation, with him, does not mean creation out of nothing; since, as the Shaikhīs maintain, the word creator is not peculiarly applicable to God alone. The Quranic verse, that " God is the best of creators ",[1] implies that there are other self-manifesting beings like God.

After the execution of ' Alī Muḥammad Bāb, Bahāullāh, one of his principal disciples who were collectively called "The First Unity", took up the mission, and proclaimed himself the originator of the new dispensation, the absent Imām whose manifesta-

[1] Sūra 23 : v. 14.

tion the Bāb had foretold. He freed the doctrine of his master from its literalistic mysticism, and presented it in a more perfected and systematised form. The Absolute Reality, according to him, is not a person; it is an eternal living Essence, to which we apply the epithets Truth and Love only because these are the highest conceptions known to us. The Living Essence manifests itself through the Universe with the object of creating in itself atoms or centres of consciousness, which as Dr. KcTaggart would say, constitute a further determination of the Hegelian Absolute. In each of these undifferentiated, simple centres of consciousness, there is hidden a ray of the Absolute Light itself, and the perfection of the spirit consists in gradually actualising, by contact with the individualising principle—matter, its emotional and intellectual possibilities, and thus discovering its own deep being—the ray of eternal Love which is concealed by its union with consciousness. The essence of man, therefore, is not reason or consciousness; it is this ray of Love—the source of all impulse to noble and unselfish action, which constitutes the real man. The influence of Mulla Ṣadrā's doctrine of the incorporeality of Imagination is here apparent. Reason, which stands higher than Imagination in the scale of evolution, is not a necessary condition, according to Mulla Ṣadrā, of immortality. In all forms of life there is an immortal spiritual part, the ray of Eternal Love, which has no necessary connection with self-consciousness or reason, and survives after the death of the body. Salvation, then, which to Buddha consists in the starving out of the mind-atoms by extinguishing desire, to Brhāullāh lies in the discovery of the essence of love whice is hidden in the atoms of consciousness themselves.[1] Both, however, agree that after death thoughts and characters of men remain, subject to other forces of a similar character, in the spiritual world, waiting for another opportunity to find a suitable physical accompaniment in order to continue the process of discovery (Bahāullāh) or destruction (Buddha). To Bahāullāh the conception of Love is higher than the conception of Will. Schopenhauer conceived reality as Will which was driven to objectification by a sinful bent eternally existing in its nature. Love or Will, according to both, is present in every atom of life; but the cause of its being there is the joy of self-expansion in the one ease, and the inexplicable evil inclination in the other. But Schopenhauer postulates certain temporal ideas in order to account for the objectification of the Primordial Will; Bahāullāh, as far as I can see, does not explain the principle according to which the self-manifestation of the Eternal Love is realised in the Universe.

[1] See Phelp's 'Abbās Effeɪ dī, chapter. "Philosophy and Psychology".

CONCLUSION

Let us now briefly sum up the results of our survey. We have seen that the Persian mind had to struggle against two different kinds of Dualism— pre-Islamic Magian Dualism, and post-Islamic Greek Dualism, though the fundamental problem of the diversity of things remains essentially the same. The attitude of the pre-Islamic Persian thinkers is thoroughly objective, and hence the results of their intellectual efforts are more or less materialistic. The Pre-Islamic thinkers, however, clearly perceived that the original Principle must be dynamically conceived. With Zoroaster both the primary spirits are "active", with Mānī the principle of Light is passive, and the principle of Darkness is aggressive. But their analysis of the various elements which constitute the Universe is ridiculously meagre ; their conception of the Universe is most defective on its statical side. There are, therefore, two weak points in their systems :—

1. Naked Dualism.
2. Lack of analysis.

The first was remedied by Islām ; the second by the introduction ef Greek Philosophy. The advent of Islām and the study of Greek philosophy, however, checked the indigenous tendency towards monistic thought; but these two forces contributed to change the objective attitude characteristic of early thinkers, and aroused the slumbering subjectivity, which eventually reached its climax in the extreme Pantheism of some of the Ṣūfī schools. Al-Fārābī endeavoured to get rid of the dualism between God and matter, by reducing matter to a mere confused perception of the spirit; the Ash'arite denied it altogether, and maintained a thorough-going Idealism. The followers of Aristotle continued to stick to their master's Prima Materia; the Ṣūfīs looked upon the material universe as a mere illusion, or a necessary "other", for the self-knowledge of God. It can, however, be safely stated that with the Ash'arite Idealism, the Persian mind, got over the foreign dualism of God and matter, and, fortified with new philosophical ideas, returned to the old dualism of light and darkness. The Shaikh-al-Ishrāq combines the objective attitude of Pre-Islamic Persian thinkers with the subjective attitude of his immediate predecessors, and restates the Dualism of Zoroaster in a much more philosophical and spiritualised form. His system recognises the claims of both the subject and the object. But all these monistic systems of thought were met by the Pluralism of Wāḥid Maḥmūd, who taught that reality is not one, but many—primary living units which combine in various ways, and gradually rise to perfection by passing through an ascending scale of forms. The reaction of Wāḥid Maḥmūd was, however, an ephemeral phenomenon. The later

Sūfīs as well as philosophers proper gradually transformed or abandoned the Neo-Platonic theory of Emanation, and in later thinkers we see a movement through Neo-Platonism towards real Platonism, which is approached by Mulla Hādī's Philosophy. But pure speculation and dreamy mysticism undergo a powerful check in Bābism which, unmindful of persecution, synthesises all the inherited philosophical and religious tendencies, and rouses the spirit to a consciousness of the stern reality of things. Though extremely cosmopolitan and hence quite unpatriotic in character, it has yet had a great influence over the Persian mind. The unmystic character and the practical tone of Bābism may have been a remote cause of the progress of recent political reform in Persia.

INDEX

A

	Page
Abbasid	38, 79
Abbās Effendi	146
Abraham	83
Abul Barakāt	95
Abu Hanīfa	79
Abu Hashim	41
Abu'l Hudhail	41
Abu l-Ma'ālī	95
Abu Mansūr	54
Abu l-Qasim	45, 95
Absolute	91, 98, 124, 145
„ Being	125, 127
Absolute	63, 90, 121
„ Being	122
„ „	127
„ „	130
„ „	131
„ Light	142
„ „	143
„ matter	103
„ quantity	103
„ unity	43
Accident	41
Activity	34
Agnostic	57, 92
Aham	89
Ahmad	41
Ahmad Shaikh	143
Agent	26
Ahriman	6, 51
Ahuramazda	4
Ahuras	3
Akbar	134
Aleppo	96

	Page
Alexander	ff 89
Alexandria	80
Allāh	122, 126
Al-Ālmidī	95
Amin	78
Animal	29
Animality	29
Annihilation	83
Anthropomorphic Hamblite	79
Appearance	8
Aristotle	23, 24, 65, 71, 97, 136, 138, 148
Aristotelian	56, 71, 97, 98, 134
Aristotelianism	92
Aryan	21, 77, 83
Al-Ash'arī	ff 40, 47, 53, 55, 64, 68, 94
Ash'arite	42, 45, 46, 52, 55, 56, 58, 60, 61, 63, 65, 66, 67, 71, 75, 79, 95, 96, 103, 148
Asrār-ul Hikam	135, 139
Assimilation	33, 34, 39
Atom	41, 58, 103
Atomic	61
Atomism	57
Atomistic	57
Al-'Attār	43
Attraction	33
Attribute	60, 75, 90, 100, 101, 144
Attributes	30, 123, 124, 128
„ Divine	131
„ of God	54
Avicenna	32, 33, 34, 35, 36, 88, 95, 139
Avicennaism	135
Averroes	23

(ii)

	Page
B	
Bābism	135, 143
Bāb, Ali Muhammad	144
Bactria	ff 89
Bādarayana	ff 125
Baghdād	39
Bahāism	143
Bahāullīh	144, 146
Bahral-Uiūm	ff 89
Bākū	89
Bāqilānī	55
St. Bartholomew	49
Al-Basīr Joseph	41
Basrā	39, 43, 53
Bashshār ibn Burd	79
Bāyazid of Bistām	89
Beautiful	133
Beauty	32, 33, 34, 89, 90, 133
„ Eternal	34, 88
Being	5, 57, 125, 131
„ Manifestation	132
Beloved	34
Benefactor	122
Barkeley	57
Al-Birūnī	64, ff 86
Body	142
„ Ideal	142
„ Physical	142
Bradley	ff 7
Bosanquet	98
Brahma	ff 125
Browne	ff 40, 77
Budha	146
Bukhārī	67
C	
Cause	26, 28
„ Primal	24
„ Ultimate	28, 65
„ Metaphysical	136
Causation, theory of	77

	Page
Christ	42, 81
	ff 89
Christian	7, 80, 82, 94
Christianity	48, 132
Church	37, 47, 63, 143
Common sense	140, 141
Comte	47
Concept	25
Conception	141
Concepts, formation of	25
Cosmology	8, 14, 98, 103
Creation	28, 43, 50, 127, 128
„ cause of	88
„ story of	91
Creator	138
„ personal	ff 125
Creative act	28
„ agency	28
D	
Daqīqī	ff 89
Darkness	6, 8, 13, 22, 99, 104,
	137, 139, 143, 147
Dastūr Ispahāni	134
Dervish	90
Descartes	59
Determined	143
Devil	13, 18, 51
Dhauq	98
Dhūl-Nūn	46
Ding-an-Sick	121, 122
Diogenes	17
Divine Names	124
„ Revelation	54
„ Will	61
Divinīty	49, 124, 125, 132
Dogma	61
Dogmatism	96
Dozy	77
Druj-Ahriman	4
Dualism	3, 18, 22, 94
„ Greek	147
„ Magian	147
„ Naked	147
„ Vieled	143

	Page		Page
Dualism of Zoroaster	148	Free will	54

E

G

Effects	28	Gelan	89
Elements	28	Al-Ghazāli	58, 59, 60, 62,
Emanation	88, 135, 136		94, 95, 96
Enneads	22	Gnostic	7, 82
Erdmann	ff 6, ff 7, 95	God	4, 5, 7, 9, 18, 26, 27, 28,
Eseence	30, 65, 69, 72, 74, 90,		40, 41, 42, 43, 44, 49, 51, 52,
	98, 122, 124, 131, 132, 136,		54, 55, 56, 57, 58, 60, 61, 62,
	138, 141, 144, 145		65, 70, 71, 85, 88, 89, 90, 92,
Eternal	27, 88, 90, 105,		121, 122, 124, 126, 127,
	126, 143, 146		130, 131, 132, 133, 137, 142,
Eternity	27, 93		144, 148
Evil	8, 9, 133	Greek	18, 38, 39, 63, 82,
Evolution	91		95, 147
Existence	25, 70, 72, 74,	Growth	33, 84
	90, 133, 144		
Existent	74, 74		
Existential	73		### H
External	34		
Externality	74	Hādī	138, 139, 141, 142, 143
		Hambalite	79
### F		Hamilton	68
		Hanafite	79, 134
Fadl	41	Harrān	22
Fakhar-al-Dīn Rāzī	54	Harūṭ	78
Fanā	83	Hearing	140
Fanaticism	49	Heavens	105
Al-Fārabī	23, 95, 148	Hegel	91, 121, 125, 126
Farawashi	9	Hegelian	132, 145
Fatalism	54	Hellenic	21
Al-Fauz-al-Asghar	24	Herbart	93
Fichte	47	Hir-Bud	134
Finite	87	Hikmat-al-Ain	65
Fire	13, 17	Hikmat-al-Ishrāq	ff 99
First	122		
First Intellect	50	### I	
Fixity	74		
Flaccus	80	Ibn Arabī	132
Form	27	,, Ashras	45
Formation	142	,, Haithum	64
Freedom	132	,, Hambal	79
Free	143	,, Hazm	6, ff 41, 43, ff 47, ff 61
Free thought	47	,, Jauzi	61

,, Maskawaih	23, 24, 26, 27, 28, 30	
,, Mubārak	67, 74	
,, Mu'tamir	44	
,, Taimiyya	82, 93	
Ideas, doctrine of	139	
Ideas, Preserver of	141	
Ideal Existence	73	
Idealism	57, 65, 91, 95, 121, 124, 148	
Idealist	68, 70, 72	
Identity	15, 30, 40, 85	
,, of the known and the knower	144	
Ikhwān-al-Safā	46	
Illuminations	100	
Imagination	25, 141, 145	
Immortal	142	
Immortality	92, 145	
Imām, Absent	144	
Imāmat	48	
Immanence	126	
Immanent	126	
Immaterial	25	
Immovable	25, 138	
Impersonal	92	
Inanimate	33	
Indeterminate	33	
Indiscernible	15	
Individual	26, 35, 100	
Intellect	100, 105, 126, 141	
Intellectualism	46, 59	
Intelligence	29	
Infinite	57, 90, 133, 138	
Invisible	86	
Islam	13, 47, 80, 82, 96, 147	
Islamic dogma	96	
,, life	77	
,, Rationalism	39	
,, Saints	80	
Ismāīlian	47, 48	
Ismāīlianism	46, 49	
Iswara	ff 125	
Al-Ishrāqī	59, 62, 94, 96	

J

Jacobi	47, 79
Al-Jāhiz	42, 45, 53
Al-Jīlī	121, 123, 126
Al-Jubbā-i	53

K

Kalām	40
Kant	57, 79, 121, 128
Kapila	128
Al-Kātibī	65, 71, 73, 74, 75
Kāzim, Hāji	144
Khalq	50
Khurāsān	78
Al-Kindi	ff 23
Kingdom, animal	34, 105
,, mineral	105
,, vegetable	105
Knowledge	13, 25, 36, 60, 72, 87, 88, 98, 102, 121, 130, 132, 144
,, Higher	ff 125
,, of unseen	86
Knowability	74
Known	70 144
Knower	144
Kundalini, doctrine of	86

L

the Last	122
Law, Islamic	134
Leibniz	15, 93
Libertarianism	54
Life	92
Light	6, 8, 9, ff 10, 11, 13, 22, 63, 87, 98, 99, 100, 137, 143, 145, 147
,, absolute	139
,, abstract	100, 101, 104
,, accidental	101, 102
,, conscious	100

Light, primal	85, 101, 104	Monistic	148, 93
Logic	95, 98	Monotheism	18, 38, 39, 57
Lotze	57	Monotheists	60
Love	32, 33, 34, 83, 89, 138, 144, 145, 146	Monotheistic	87, 93
		Motion	24, 25, 105, 138, 140
		Movable	138

M

		Mover	25, 138
		Multiplicity	25, 46, 47, 139, 142
Macdonald	48	Muʻtazila	40, 43
Magi	5	Muʻtazilaism	39, 45, 53
Magian	4, 99	Mysticism	95. 145
Māhiyyat	45, 55		
Majd yīlī	96		
Al-Mālik	79, 96	**N**	
Mālikite	79		
Mānī	11, 13, 14, 15, 147,	Nafs	35
Manichean	51	Nahāwand	21
Manifestation	34, 125	Names	123
Maʻruf Karkhī	88	Nasafī	90
Mary	52	Nature	4, 15, 121
Materialism	38	Naturalism	46
Materialist	26	Nazzīm	41, 42, 61, 94
Matter	25, 27, 30, 148	Negative	75
„ theory of	45	Neo-Platonism	22, 77, 80, 81, 92, 136
„ indeterminate	33		
Mātarīdiyya	54	Neo-Platonists	22, 92, 135
Mazdak	11, 17	Neo-Platonic	37, 88, 91
Mazdakite	16,	Nicholson	77
McTaggart	145	Nirvāna	83
Mimūn	78, 79	Non-eternal	27
Mansūr	89	Non-existence	25, 27, 73
Man	4, 24, 28, 143	Non-existent	27, 43, 73, 74, 75
Mānī	16, 147	Nothing	27, 74
Mathematics	98, 137	Nūr-i-Qāhir	98
Māyā	15, 124		
Metaphysical	55, 83		
Metaphysics	38, 58, 87, 95, 98	**O**	
Metempsychosis	34, 35		
Medium	143, 144		
Memory	141	Objects, External	30
Mereiful	123	Ojectification	61
Mercy	125, 126	One	122, 138
Merx	77	Oneness	124, 125, 127, 133
Mird	9, ff 10, 140, 147	Ontology	98
Mishkātal Anwār	62	Orthodox	40, 58, 59, 61
Monism	80, ff 125	Originator	126

P

	Page
Pantheism	47, 88, 93, 126, 148
Pautheistic	60, 89
Patanjali	ff 86
Percept	26
Perception	25, 30, 142
Perfection	33, 122, 133, 138
Perfect Man	131
Perfecting	140
Permanence	92
Perpetuating	140
Personal	30
Personality	61
Philosophers	22
Philosophy	6, 21, 23, 39, 48, 49, 51, 58, 62, 63, 94, 98, 134, 136, 137, 143, 147
Plotinus	22, 80, 81, 136
Plato	8, 9, ff 10, 22, 23, 89, 97, 136, 138, 139, 142
Platonism	135
Pluralism	148
Plurality	41, 50, 138
Pluralistic	93
Positive	74
Positivism	63
Post-Islamic	135
Prakriti	128
Pre-existence	36
Pre-existential	43
Pre-Islamic	147, 148
Prima-Materia	65, 102, 148
Primordial	99, 146
Principle Divine	40
Prophet	60, 62, 63
Providence	126
Psychology	64, 98, 139
Pure Being	122, 125
Purification	142
Pyrrho	81

Q

Qadari	ff 40
Qadi Iyad	61
Qalb	130
Quality	56, 90, 102
Qur'an	50, 51, 55, 63, 82, 83, 84, 85, 132
Quranic Standpoint	84
Sh-Al-Qushairi	79, 88
Qutb-ul-Din	54

R

Rationalism	38, 40, 42, 45, 48, 52, 54, 61, 62, 63, 78, 79, 95
Rationalist	42, 43
Rationalists	49, 54, 65, 94, 143
Rationalistic	79
Razi	24
Al-Razi	59, 67, 74, 95, 96
Reaction	46, 64
Real	63, 136, 137, 138, 139, 144
Realisation	86
Reality	8, 87, 88, 90, 92, 93, 94, 134, 139, 144, 145
Realism	65, 124,
Realist	67
Reason	9, 47, 48, 50, 79, 137, 142, 145
Religion, Shi'ah	143
Religious life	80
Reproduction	33, 34
Resurrection	74
Rumi	82, 89

S

Sacred Fire	89
Sadra Mulla	134, 135, 143, 144, 145
Saffarid	78
Salah-al-Din, Sultan	96
Salvation	145
Samaned	78
Samarqand	54
Samkara	ff 125
Sankhya	ff 86
Sanskrit	18, ff 86

	Page		Page
Sarkhsī	23	Stoicism	81
Sat	ff 125	Substance	27, 33, 43, 56, 57, 60, 75, 90, 100, 102, 103, 144
Scepticism	38, 39, 62, 79, 81, 95, 98	Substances Primary,	29
Schlegel	47	Substratum	30
Schleiermacher	47, 79	Subzwīr	135
Schopenhauer	128, 146	Sūfī	87, 89
Science, Physical	136	,, Cosmology	ff 10
Search after the Unseen	85	,, Pantheism	60
Self	137	,, Schools	148
,, Consciousness	34	,, Thought	92
,, Knowledge	101	Sūfīs	88, 130, 138, 149
,, Recognition	91	Sūfīism	46, 48, 51, 52, 60, 62, 76, 77, 80, 82, 83, 86, 98, 134
Semitic	21, 77, 78, 82, 83, 88	Summation of qualities	98
Sensations	25		
Senses	29, 140	**T**	
,, Internal	35		
,, External	35		
Shadow	137	Tafra	43
Shāfiite	79	Tahirīd	78
Al-Shafi'ī	79	Tamas	15
Shahāb-al-Dīn	95, 96	Tartar	134
Shāh Abbās	94	Temperament	34
Shahristānī	ff 43, 51	Thales	4
Shaikh-al-Ishrāq	96, 148	Theology	61, 100
Shaqīq Balkhī	87	,, Islamic	62
Sharīf, Mīr Sayyīd	88	Theological	55
Shaikhīs	144	Theory of Knowledge	70
Shīrāz	94, 134, 143	Things	139
Shibli	29, 61	Thought	25, 79, 87, 93, 97
Shi'ite	ff 40	Transcendental	98
,, Religion	47	Transformation	34
Shu'ūbiyya	78	,, of feeling	82
Sight	140	,, of will	82
Simplicius	17	Transmigration	142
Soul	29, 30, 34, 35, 36, 85, 98	Trinity, Doctrine of	130
,, animal	140	Truth	145
,, human	140	Twins, Primal	5
,, vegetative	140		
,, Heavenly	140	**U**	
,, Earthly	140		
Speculation	82	Ultimate	25, 26, 90, 92, 94
Speculative	83	,, cause	28
Spinoza	93	,, reality	52, 87
Spirit	141, 142	Unconsciousness	127
Spitta	53	Uncaused	71

Uncreatable	123
Understanding	126
Unknowable	70
Unknowability	127
Unknown	133
Unlimited	133
Unity	17, 41, 51, 138, 139, 142
,, Absolute	135
,, the First	144
,, Primal	50
Universal	26, 48, 51, 100, 142
Universe	17, 43, 44, 50, 51, 52, 56, 57, 62, 82, 83, 87, 88, 93, 100, 102, 104, 105, 121, 122, 125, 131, 132, 137, 138, 139, 144, 145, 147
Unseen	84, 85
Ustādhīs	78

V

Vedānta	77, 124, ff 125, 130
Vedāntic	87
Vedāntist	15, 82, 86, 89
Vegetable	33
Vegetative	29
Visible	86
Von-Kremer	ff 40, ff 47 77, 87

W

Wāhid Mahmūd	93, 148
Whittaker	92
Will	42, 57, 87, 132, 136, 144, 146
Wisdom	13, 84
Wordsworth	79
Wujūd	55

Z

Al-Zāhir	96
Zendīks	78
Zoroaster	37, 50, 135, 147, 148
Zoroastrian	51, 89, 99
Zoroastrianism	134

Printed in the United States
100259LV00003B/297/A